THE PSYCHOLOGIST-MANAGER JOURNAL

Volume 9, Number

THE PSYCHOLOGIST-MANAGER JOURNAL, 2006, 9(2), 67–69
Copyright © 2006 by the Society of Psychologists in Management

Douglas W. Bray, PhD: A Dedication

Deborah E. Rupp
University of Illinois at Urbana-Champaign

It is with great honor, respect, and sadness that I write this dedication to Douglas W. Bray, who died May 9, 2006. This special issue of *The Psychologist-Manager Journal* showcases research exploring the global validity of developmental assessment centers. The research presented herein was made possible by the SIOP Foundation's Douglas W. Bray and Ann Howard award to support research on assessment centers and managerial/leadership development. If it were not for Dr. Bray, there would not have been such an award, there would not be this set of articles, and there likely would not be assessment centers as we know them today. Indeed, Doug Bray was a legendary pioneer who has changed the landscape of industrial/organizational psychology. Both Doug Bray and his wife Ann Howard have been long-time members of the Society of Psychologists in Management.

In 1956, Doug Bray was asked by AT&T to conduct a longitudinal research project which traced the development of managers throughout their careers. In order to assess and track managerial competence, Dr. Bray developed the first private industry assessment center. In 1968, Bray assisted Bill Byham in developing an assessment center at J.C. Penney. With the publication of Bray and Grant's important *Psychological Monographs* paper in 1966, which introduced the AC method to science, and Byham's influential *Harvard Business Review* paper in 1970, which introduced the method to practice, both the scholarly and applied worlds became very interested in assessment centers as a serious management tool. In 1973, Bray and Byham co-founded the International Congress on Assessment Center Methods, as well as Development Dimensions International, a now world-wide consulting firm known for service offerings in the area of assessment and development. Dr. Bray was on the original taskforce that developed the *Guidelines and Ethical Considerations for Assessment Center Operations*, first published in 1975 and now entering its fifth edition. These *Guidelines* serve as the major professional standards for assessment center practices. The research Bray conducted at AT&T and the Bell System continued for 25 years. He was joined by Ann Howard in these efforts, and together, Bray and Howard broke significant new ground in the science and practice of assessment centers. Bray's original *Management Progress Study*

(1964) is one of the most referenced projects in the history of Industrial/Organizational Psychology. The chronicle of his life's work, *Managerial Lives in Transition: Advancing Age and Changing Times* (1988) by Howard and Bray is a treatise on that which we seek to understand as a field: the interaction of dynamic individual qualities and dynamic situational factors in influencing the development of the professional lives of people over time.

The impact of Doug Bray's work has been staggering. There are over 50,000 operational assessment centers world wide, with the number of individuals being assessed annually in the millions. Dr. Bray published over 60 books and scholarly papers. He received the Society for Industrial and Organizational Psychology (SIOP) Distinguished Professional Contributions Award, the American Psychological Foundation Gold Medal award for Life Achievement in the Application of Psychology, and the Distinguished Psychologist in Management Award given annually by the Society for Psychologists in Management (SPIM). Also evidencing his unyielding service to the field are his terms as SIOP President, APA Ethics Committee Chair, and President of the Board of Directors of the American Board of Professional Psychology.

Doug Bray had a command and presence like no other. In the words of Dr. Bray's close colleague (and my mentor) Dr. George C. Thornton (who learned the assessment center method directly from Bray at AT&T/DDI in the 1970s), "Doug was a stickler for high-quality research, a cheerleader for younger professionals, a curmudgeon who let you know if he disagreed with you, and a person who you wanted for a friend but feared and respected as an opponent." I personally met Dr. Bray only once, at the last International Congress on Assessment Centers he was able to attend. As a young scholar, I will never forget this career moment. Ann Howard introduced me to Doug as "a next generation I/O Psychologist" doing new and different assessment center research in the spirit of their landmark longitudinal research conducted across the decades. Dr. Bray took my hand tightly, pulled me toward him, looked at me directly, and said very quietly yet sternly, "Keep it up."

We plan to keep it up, and hope that the research presented herein will catalyze continued thinking, dialog, and empirical investigation into the assessment, development, and understanding of managers and leaders; and that as a field, we can continue pushing Doug Bray's legacy forward. This issue of *The Psychologist-Manager Journal* is dedicated to his memory.

References

Bray, D. W. (1964). The management progress study. *American Psychologist, 19*, 419–420.
Bray, D. W., & Grant, D. L. (1966). The assessment center in the measurement of potential for business management. *Psychological Monographs: General & Applied, 80*(17), 27.

Byham, W. C. (1970). Assessment centers for spotting future managers. *Harvard Business Review,* *48*(4), 150–168.

International Task Force on Assessment Center Guidelines. (2000). Guidelines and ethical considerations for assessment center operations. *Public Personnel Management, 29,* 315–331.

Howard, A., & Bray, D.W. (1988). *Managerial lives in transition: Advancing age and changing times.* New York: Guilford Press.

THE PSYCHOLOGIST-MANAGER JOURNAL, 2006, 9(2), 71–74

 INTRODUCTION

Introduction to Special Issue: Developmental Assessment Centers

William D. Siegfried, Jr.
Department of Psychology
The University of North Carolina at Charlotte

The history of assessment centers is widely known. Their earliest use was in the militaries of various countries to select officers and, later, spies (Kello, in press-a), but perhaps the best-known civilian application was the selection and development of managers at AT&T (Howard & Bray, 1988). Assessment centers typically involve a series of exercises or simulations that elicit behaviors on dimensions that have been shown to be important on the job. For example, candidates may engage in a leaderless group discussion in which their ability to influence others can be judged. Although a manager may never engage in a leaderless group discussion once on the job, the ability to influence others is an important dimension that might predict success in a variety of managerial roles. Role-playing and in-baskets are other widely used simulations (Kello, in press-b). A well-designed assessment center (see International Task Force on Assessment Center Guidelines, 2000) can yield rich information on job-related skills that should make it easy to spot the right candidates to hire or promote.

In fact, assessment centers do seem to be good, if not perfect, predictors. Several meta-analyses (see Arthur, Day, McNelly, & Edens, 2003; Gaugler, Rosenthal, Thornton, & Bentson, 1987) have shown impressive criterion-related validities for overall candidate ratings and for many separate dimensions. Also, because the exercises can be clearly linked to the facets of job performance, assessment centers are perceived to be fair (Kello, in press-b).

Correspondence should be sent to William D. Siegfried, Jr., Department of Psychology, The University of North Carolina at Charlotte, 9201 University City Blvd., Charlotte, NC 28223-001. E-mail: wsiegfrd@email.uncc.edu

In addition to being used as a textbook example of good practice for selection, assessment centers are discussed as a way to develop employees, and this aspect is undoubtedly true. An assessment center generates a lot of data about a person's performance on key job dimensions. Although this information is used to make a yes–no decision, it can also be a source of feedback for the individual.

However, although this dual role is often mentioned, the majority of the research has concentrated on selection, and much less is known about the effectiveness of assessment centers as a developmental device. It cannot be assumed that because assessment centers work as predictors, they will also be valuable in development, because the purposes of these two activities are fundamentally different. In selection, the goal is to find candidates who possess the appropriate skills and then to slot them into jobs; in development, the goal is to find a person in a job and determine which skills are lacking. Taking a standard assessment center designed for selection and using it for development may not be appropriate. The purpose of this issue of the journal is to begin to fill that gap in knowledge about using assessment centers for development.

In the first article, Rupp, Snyder, Gibbons, and Thornton outline the general issues in developmental assessment centers and highlight the importance of choosing dimensions for development. Because the fundamental purpose is to foster development, the dimensions assessed must be those on which improvement is possible. As the authors point out, the important dimensions are those on which people are likely to change, whereas in traditional assessment we are trying to assess traits that we assume (and hope) will not change. Additionally, people being assessed must believe that change on a dimension is possible.

The second article, by Gibbons, Rupp, Snyder, Holub, and Woo, begins to define what those dimensions might be. This is an empirical investigation where managers rated common dimensions on their importance for successful management performance but also indicated their beliefs about the developability of those dimensions. The result suggests where efforts may be productive in promoting individual change and related organizational success.

Shifting the emphasis from selection to development allows one to include dimensions that might be seen as being important for success but not necessarily used for selection. Examples that come to mind include "fitting in," "citizenship," or "getting along with others." One such dimension emerging from this study was fairness.

The third study, by Gibbons, Rupp, Kim, and Woo, tests the robustness and generalizability of the dimensions with a Korean managerial sample. As might be expected, there were some differences between the two countries, but there was overlap as well. It might be easy to dismiss this article as being irrelevant for all those not working with a Korean sample, but to do so would obscure two points. First, the overlap in the dimensions deemed important, taken with other studies, such as Arthur et al. (2003), suggests that there may be a fairly small number of dimensions that predict successful management performance across settings. Second, an examination of the differences between U.S. managers and Korean managers raises some interesting questions about American practices. Unless one is working in Korea, the question of how Korean managers are different is merely interesting. Turned around, however, the question becomes, how are Americans different from managers in other parts of the world? What does it say about Americans when it is found that they care less about interpersonal relationships and organizational knowledge and more about communication skills? Does this imply that U.S. managers think that it is acceptable to not get along and to not know their jobs as long as they can talk a good game? I will not overinterpret the data any further, but the point is that by studying what successful management looks like from the perspective of different cultures, one might find that some of the nation's valued practices are harmful idiosyncrasies.

The fourth study, by Rupp, Baldwin, and Bashshur, is an application piece that shows how one nontraditional dimension—in this case, workplace fairness—might be assessed and developed. The article presents a comprehensive review of the justice and fairness literature but then derives specific management behaviors from the key concepts. These behaviors, in turn, can be assessed, and the authors suggest exercises that form the basis of a developmental assessment center. Justice is often seen as a concept, but this article shows how it may be seen as a behavioral management competency suitable for training.

The final piece in the sequence, by Rupp, Gibbons, Baldwin, Snyder, Spain, Woo, Brummel, Sims, and Kim, is an empirical validation study of two developmental assessment centers. Information is presented about participant reactions, within-program learning, and behavior back on the job as rated by subordinates. Taken as a whole, the results offer encouragement for the use of this technique, although the authors do call for some caution in interpreting the results.

On a broad scale, it is clear that assessment is becoming part of the public dialogue. In the public schools, the No Child Left Behind Act has brought the issues of accuracy and fairness into the public domain. Those who work in higher education face increased scrutiny of faculty performance, often through newly established procedures for posttenure review. Many psychologist-managers are committed to leadership development, as trainers or consultants, and some currently thrive as coaches, a job that 20 years ago was confined to athletic arenas. Developmental assessment centers might be used to improve practice in all of these areas. Will psychologist-managers see the day when all aspiring MBA students are assessed to determine their real potential as managers? Will their school children be given the opportunity to show their strengths on dimensions other than those measured on standardized tests? Will one among them develop a freestanding assessment center to serve clients from diverse organizations? Psychologist-managers are compelled by their training and ethics to use only the best and most valid assessment techniques—would assessment centers be among those? These are questions that I can pose; the articles that follow begin to provide some answers.

ACKNOWLEDGMENTS

The research presented in this issue was produced in part with support from the first Douglas W. Bray and Ann Howard Award, which is administered by the Society for Industrial and Organizational Psychology. The award supports research to advance the understanding of assessment center techniques and managerial or leadership development.

Alyssa Mitchell Gibbons and Deborah Rupp deserve credit for this issue. Not only do their names appear on most of the articles, but they also took the lead in pulling the entire series together into a coherent whole. They are the driving force behind the finished product.

REFERENCES

Arthur, W., Jr., Day, E. A., McNelly, T. L., & Edens, P. S. (2003). A meta-analysis of the criterion-related validity of assessment center dimensions. *Personnel Psychology, 56,* 125–154.

Gaugler, B. B., Rosenthal, D. B., Thornton, G. C., III, & Bentson, C. (1987). Meta-analysis of assessment center validity. *Journal of Applied Psychology, 72,* 493–511.

Howard, A., & Bray, D. W. (1988). *Managerial lives in transition: Advancing age and changing times.* New York: Guilford.

International Task Force on Assessment Center Guidelines. (2000). Guidelines and ethical considerations for assessment center operations. *Public Personnel Management, 29,* 315–331.

Kello, J. (in press-a). Assessment center. In S. G. Rogelberg (Ed.), *The encyclopaedia of industrial and organizational psychology.* Thousand Oaks, CA: Sage.

Kello, J. (in press-b). Assessment center methods. In S. G. Rogelberg (Ed.), *The encyclopaedia of industrial and organizational psychology.* Thousand Oaks, CA: Sage.

THE PSYCHOLOGIST-MANAGER JOURNAL, 2006, 9(2), 75–98

 I. DEVELOPMENTAL ASSESSMENT
CENTERS

What Should Developmental Assessment Centers be Developing?

Deborah E. Rupp
Department of Psychology
University of Illinois at Urbana-Champaign

Lori A. Snyder
Department of Psychology
University of Oklahoma

Alyssa Mitchell Gibbons
Department of Psychology
University of Illinois at Urbana-Champaign

George C. Thornton III
Department of Psychology
Colorado State University

This article raises an important and seldom discussed question for those who design and implement developmental assessment centers (DACs): Are the dimensions traditionally assessed in managerial assessment centers also the most appropriate for DACs? Dimensions in DACs are often borrowed directly from traditional assessment centers, with little consideration of whether, to what extent, or how development can be expected to take place. In this article, we explain the necessity of considering development, and we discuss the importance of both objective and perceived de-

Correspondence should be sent to Deborah E. Rupp, Department of Psychology and Institute of Labor and Industrial Relations, University of Illinois at Urbana-Champaign, 603 East Daniel Street, Champaign, IL 61820. E-mail: derupp@uiuc.edu

velopability. We further discuss the concept of a continuum of developability and offer recommendations for DAC researchers and for practitioners seeking to determine the appropriateness of dimensions for DAC programs.

Assessment centers have a long, rich, and successful history. Hundreds of thousands of employees have been assessed using this method, and hundreds of research studies have been conducted on the use of assessment centers (Howard, 1997). Indeed, it is generally accepted that assessment centers have adequate criterion-related validity (Gaugler, Rosenthal, Thornton, & Bentson, 1987; Hunter & Hunter, 1984; Schmidt & Hunter, 1998) and incremental validity above that of cognitive ability tests, supervisor ratings (Chan, 1996), and personality tests (Goffin, Rothstein, & Johnston, 1996). The majority of this research has been conducted on traditional assessment centers (ACs), which are used for the purpose of making selection, placement, or promotion decisions and diagnosing training needs (Kudisch et al., 2001; Spychalski, Quiñones, Gaugler, & Pohley, 1997).

A more recent application of the AC method that is gaining popularity in practice (Kudisch et al., 2001) is to use ACs as a tool for fostering employees' professional development. ACs used for this purpose are referred to as *developmental assessment centers* (DACs) in that they serve the dual purpose of assessment and development (Iles & Forster, 1994; Joiner, 2002; Kudisch, Ladd, & Dobbins, 1997). Survey research indicates that upward of 40% of the operational ACs in practice today are of a developmental nature (Ballantyne & Povah, 2004; Constable, 1999; Spychalski et al., 1997), and many more human resource professionals are considering implementing such programs (U.K. Industrial Society, 1996).

Despite their popularity, a paucity of research exists on the effectiveness of DACs. The popularity of the method appears to rest almost entirely on the reputation of traditional ACs, which are different from DACs in many fundamental ways (see Table 1). Therefore, some authors have questioned whether researchers can generalize their knowledge about ACs to the DAC method, and they have called for research exploring the effectiveness of DACs across a variety of organizations, industries, and cultures (Carrick & Williams, 1999; Thornton & Rupp, 2005). They note that, for the most part, the design principles and best practices established for traditional ACs (e.g., Arthur, Woehr, & Maldegen, 2000; International Task Force on Assessment Center Guidelines, 2000) have not been empirically shown to be appropriate for DACs but, rather, have been generally assumed to be so. Given the differences between the methods, researchers and practitioners who develop DACs must consider whether following the traditional AC model is the most effective way to produce the intended development.

One significant assumption that has broad implications for all aspects of DAC development is that the constructs that have traditionally been assessed in selection ACs are also those that can be most effectively assessed and developed in a DAC context (Thornton & Rupp, 2005). These constructs, often referred to in the AC

TABLE 1
Differences Between Traditional and Developmental Assessment Centers

	Traditional Assessment Center	Developmental Assessment Center
Purpose	Assessment Human resource decision making	Assessment and development Transfer of training
Experience	Diagnostic	Experiential learning, self-reflection, performance improvement
Assessee's role	Assessee	Active learner
Focus	Overall performance	Dimension performance Improvement
Dimensions	Not always transparent Stable abilities	Extremely transparent Developable knowledge and skills
Feedback	Pass/fail, given upon completion	Extensive, given at multiple time points; detailed, behavior-based, high-quality action plans
Predictive validity evidence	Overall rating or dimension ratings predict future success on the job	Dimension proficiency increases over time as a result of the developmental assessment center and subsequent developmental activities

Note. From *Assessment Centers in Human Resource Management*, p. 66, by G. C. Thornton and D. E. Rupp, 2005, Mahwah, NJ: Lawrence Erlbaum Associates, Inc. Copyright 2005 by Lawrence Erlbaum Associates, Inc. Reprinted with permission.

field as *behavioral dimensions*, are generally chosen for their relevance to the target job (based on job analysis; International Task Force on Assessment Center Guidelines, 2000). Some research has investigated the degree to which different dimensions are predictive of subsequent job performance (e.g., Arthur, Day, McNelly, & Edens, 2003). For selection purposes, these are logical criteria. For developmental purposes, however, there are other factors to consider. Our purpose in the present article is not to argue that the criterion of job relevance is inappropriate for DACs but, rather, to argue that it is insufficient. Dimensions for DACs should be based on dimensions that can be expected to provide a reasonable return on investment in terms of performance improvement. Theory suggests that not all dimensions are equally developable (e.g., Brush & Licata, 1983; Waters, 1980) and not all training methods are equally effective for all skills (Arthur, Bennett, Edens, & Bell, 2003). Some highly relevant managerial competencies may not be well suited to development via a DAC. What is needed is an investigation of the dimensions most relevant for development and the dimensions most amenable to development using a DAC intervention.

If DACs are to be effective means of improving managerial performance, they must be designed in ways that make development most likely—that is, focusing on competencies that are important for success, amenable to change, and believed by the manager to be improvable. Though it is critical to examine the actual, or "objective," developability of particular dimensions, it is also important to consider participants' implicit theories about the developability of dimensions, because such theories have the potential to affect development itself (Dweck & Leggett, 1988). In the following sections, we describe DACs and behavioral dimensions in detail; we then discuss relevant research and theory regarding objective and perceived developability and present a three-stage process for DAC dimension choice. We then consider the question of appropriate dimensions from the opposite angle: Are there dimensions that are not typically assessed in selection ACs that might be quite effectively developed in DACs? We conclude by presenting a call not only to researchers to address several pressing questions regarding developability but also to practitioners to make development the central principle of their DACs. This final section intends to provide managers with some practical guidance when faced with the challenge of what dimensions to include in a DAC.

THE DAC PROCESS

A DAC is a collection of workplace simulation exercises and other assessments that provide individuals with practice, feedback, and coaching on a set of developable behavioral dimensions found to be critical for their professional success (Thornton & Rupp, 2003, 2005). Most DACs conform to the *Guidelines and Ethical Considerations for Assessment Center Operations* (International Task Force on Assessment Center Guidelines, 2000), but there is otherwise little consensus regarding what DACs should look like. In practice, a DAC may be anything from a traditional selection center that provides feedback to a diagnostic launching pad for future development to a self-contained training intervention (Thornton & Rupp, 2005). Increasingly, however, researchers have begun to articulate the many ways in which a truly development-focused AC may differ from traditional ACs (see Table 1). Rupp, Thornton, and colleagues (Gibbons & Rupp, 2004; Rupp & Thornton, 2003; Rupp, Thornton, & Gibbons, 2004; Thornton & Rupp, 2005), influenced by the work of other AC scholars (Ballantyne & Povah, 2004; Boehm, 1985; Carrick & Williams, 1999; Engelbrecht & Fischer, 1995; Griffiths & Goodge, 1994; Jones & Whitmore, 1995; Lee, 2000; Lee & Beard, 1994), have synthesized these ideas into a potential DAC model (see Figure 1) that illustrates how a DAC might be designed to maximize opportunities for development.

As conceptualized here, a DAC need not be merely the preliminary diagnostic step at the start of an employee development program but may be a meaningful training intervention in and of itself and therefore an integral component of the development process (Carrick & Williams, 1999; Rupp & Thornton, 2003; Thornton

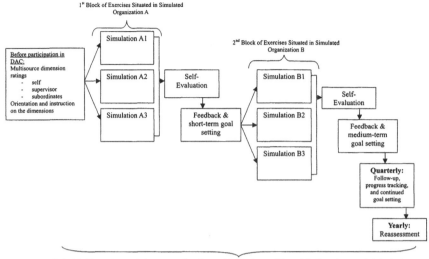

1ˢᵗ Block of Exercises Situated in Simulated
Organization A

2ⁿᵈ Block of Exercises Situated in Simulated
Organization B

FIGURE 1   Sample developmental assessment center process model. From *Assessment Centers in Human Resource Management,* p. 60, by G. C. Thornton and D. E. Rupp, 2005, Mahwah, NJ: Lawrence Erlbaum Associates, Inc. Copyright 2005 by Lawrence Erlbaum Associates, Inc.

& Rogers, 2001). To maximize learning throughout the process, a purely developmental DAC may incorporate elements such as training on the dimensions, exercises designed to maximize experiential learning, self-reflection activities, and coaching and goal setting at multiple points throughout the center. Dimensions are made completely transparent to the participants, and care is taken to create a nonthreatening learning environment where experimentation and exploration are supported. Finally, participants are encouraged to engage in further development activities following the DAC to continue improving themselves on the dimensions. If possible, follow-up contacts with participants may be made to track their progress over time and increase the maintenance and generalizability of transfer of training by reminding them of the DAC experience.

The Thornton and Rupp (2005) model is, of course, only one example of how a DAC might be designed. It does, however, highlight the growing emphasis on development in the AC literature and suggest that the DACs of the future may bear less and less resemblance to their traditional AC cousins. As Figure 1 and Table 1 illustrate, the shift from an assessment to a development focus can affect nearly every aspect of DAC design and implementation. Our concern in the present article is whether and to what extent considerations of developability should influence the choice of the behavioral dimensions to be assessed for DACs of all kinds.

BEHAVIORAL DIMENSIONS

Dimensions are defined for AC purposes as clusters of "behaviors that are specific, observable, and verifiable, and that can be reliably and logically classified together" (Thornton & Byham, 1982, p. 117). Dimensions consist of specific behaviors but are general enough to be observable across a variety of situations and tasks (International Task Force on Assessment Center Guidelines, 2000). According to the guidelines, the choice of dimensions should be based on job analysis. Research has shown that a smaller set of dimensions (e.g, three to six) is typically more effective than a larger set of dimensions (e.g., over nine; Gaugler & Thornton, 1989; Sackett & Tuzinski, 2001; Woehr & Arthur, 2003).

The choice of dimensions is critical to the overall effectiveness of any AC program. Dimensions are the currency, foundation, and building blocks of any AC. Failing to systematically identify the dimensions most appropriate for DAC programs is analogous to developing a selection system without conducting a job analysis to identify the knowledge, skills, and abilities necessary for successful job performance—one cannot lose track of the constructs being assessed and developed in the study of the method with which one assesses and develops them (Arthur, Day, et al., 2003). According to *Standards for Educational and Psychological Testing* (American Educational Research Association, American Psychological Association, & American Council on Measurement in Education, 1999), the validity of an assessment relies on the available evidence supporting its quality. For any AC, this evidence must include information supporting the job relevance of the dimensions. However, we argue that for DACs, information about the developability of the dimensions also represents critical evidence that should be considered as well.

Whether dimensions should be used in ACs at all is the topic of much debate in the research literature (e.g., Arthur et al., 2000; Lance, Lambert, Gewin, Lievens, & Conway, 2004; Lievens & Conway, 2001; Sackett & Dreher, 1982; Sackett & Tuzinski, 2001; Woehr & Arthur, 2003). Analyses of postexercise dimension ratings generally find high correlations between dimensions within the same exercise and low correlations between ratings of the same dimension measured in different exercises (for a recent meta-analysis, see Lance et al., 2004). In light of this, Lance and colleagues recommended disregarding dimensions entirely and scoring each exercise as a work sample; if the exercises are carefully designed to reflect job content, integration of overall exercise ratings should still yield high predictive validity. In their view, dimensions are not at all necessary to the success of the AC method.

Why, then, in the face of this evidence, do we persist in recommending the use of dimensions to DAC developers? One reason is that dimensions play a different role in DACs than in traditional ACs, and it is not clear that they can be so easily dispensed with. Lance and colleagues (2004) were concerned primarily with traditional selection or promotion centers. Aggregating overall exercise scores may be an adequate means of arriving at an overall assessment rating, but DACs generally provide feedback at the dimension level. It is not clear whether giving exercise-based feedback is likely to improve on-the-job performance (as opposed to simply improving performance in future ACs), and the existing literature suggests few alternative bases for feedback. Attempts to structure traditional ACs around "managerial functions" have not been particularly successful (Joyce, Thayer, & Pond, 1994). Dimensions are the traditional currency of ACs and of job analysis and performance appraisal, because they allow discrete behaviors to be clustered into meaningful categories (Thornton & Byham, 1982). Such categories are helpful in organizing and processing feedback; presenting a long list of individual behaviors can quickly become overwhelming for participants. Regardless of whether dimensions as they are typically used are the optimal set of categories, empirical research is needed to identify alternatives.

Further, evidence exists that dimension ratings are more distinct when judgments are aggregated across exercises (Robie, Osburn, Morris, Etchegaray, & Adams, 2000; Woehr & Arthur, 2003) and that across-exercise dimension ratings are meaningfully related to performance outcomes (Arthur, Day, et al., 2003). More generally, DAC practitioners must keep in mind that the quality of the DAC is highly dependent on the ability of assessors and administrators to provide distinct and meaningful feedback on each dimension. Many design choices can be made in such a way as to make this feat more likely, such as choosing dimensions that have little conceptual overlap (Thornton & Byham, 1982; Thornton & Rupp, 2005), writing clear behavioral definitions that leave little room for confusion, and designing exercises in such a way as to encourage dimension-relevant behavior (Haaland & Christiansen, 2002). We encourage practitioners to remain abreast of research developments in this area, because the body of knowledge concerning DACs continues to expand.

Identifying job-relevant dimensions for use in managerial DACs is not an easy task, but it is at least a well-documented one. A wealth of research and practical advice is available to the practitioner conducting a job analysis (e.g., Chen, Carsten, & Krauss, 2003; McCormick, 1976; Sanchez & Levine, 2001), and guidelines for translating job analytic data into AC dimensions are also well established (International Task Force on Assessment Center Guidelines, 2000; Thornton & Byham, 1982; Thornton & Rupp, 2005). There is also a fair amount of published research that suggests how various dimensions are relevant for managerial success across organizations, industries, and levels (Gaugler, Bentson, & Pohley, 1990). This research is consistent with the general managerial taxonomies found in the broader job performance literature (e.g., Borman & Brush, 1993; Tett, Guterman, Bleier, & Murphy, 2000).

The job analysis process usually results in far more dimensions than can be measured within a single AC; consequently, the AC designer must identify the most appropriate subset of dimensions, given the context of the overall organization and the purpose of the center (Thornton & Byham, 1982). For traditional ACs, in which the primary purpose is selection or promotion, dimensions are commonly selected based on the degree to which they predict future performance (Thornton & Rupp, 2005). Over time, a substantial body of research has developed regarding which AC dimensions have been most predictive of performance (Byham, 1970; Gaugler et al., 1987; Hardison & Sackett, 2004; Hunter & Hunter, 1984; Schmitt, Noe, Meritt, & Fitzgerald, 1984; Thornton & Byham, 1982). Practitioners can draw on this literature and integrate it with their own job analyses to identify the dimensions that can be expected to best predict performance for the job in question.

For DACs, however, the question of dimension choice becomes more challenging. The job analysis for a DAC is no different from that for a selection or promotion AC, but the fundamental difference in the purpose of DACs and ACs implies that the subset of dimensions chosen for one may not necessarily be appropriate for the other. Whereas ACs are concerned with prediction of future performance, DACs are concerned with providing useful feedback and fostering development. As such, DACs require dimensions on which it is possible to improve, given some amount of time and effort (Thornton & Byham, 1982; Thornton & Rogers, 2001; Thornton & Rupp, 2005). Stable traits[1] are often used for prediction (i.e, in selection ACs) precisely because they are unlikely to change (Howard & Bray, 1988). Though participants may find it helpful or informative to receive feedback on such dimensions (cf. Jones & Whitmore, 1995; Thornton & Byham, 1982), it is difficult to see how this feedback will lead to improvement in performance (Thornton & Rupp, 2005). At a minimum, such feedback should make the stability of the dimension explicit so that the recipient can turn his or her efforts to working around the deficiency instead of trying fruitlessly to overcome it. This, however, requires a clear understanding of the developability of the dimensions.

DEVELOPABILITY

The idea that different skills can be learned at different rates is intuitive, and research has long supported this notion, at least with respect to basic skills (e.g., McGeoch, 1929). At present, the available training and development literature offers many general principles of learning (e.g., Salas & Cannon-Bowers, 2001; Wexley & Baldwin, 1986) and many descriptions of successful development inter-

---

[1]We use the terms *trait*, *traitlike*, and *stable* with much caution. To conform with the guidelines, all dimensions must be defined in behavioral terms. Thus, even cognitive and personality traits need to be defined behaviorally if assessed in an AC context. Many personality researchers use behavioral definitions (e.g., Buss & Craik, 1983), even for traits that are believed to represent relatively stable individual differences. Our concern here is with the learnability of the behaviors associated with a given trait or dimension label; thus, the critical word in this phrase is not *trait* but *stable*.

ventions but only a few comprehensive, well-delineated theories about which skills may be developed by what means. Hellervik, Hazucha, and Schneider (1992) proposed a model of behavior changeability. This model posits that changeability is driven by the complexity of the behavior to be learned. That is, complex skills—according to Hellervik et al., those strongly correlated with cognitive ability—are more difficult to learn than simple skills, and specific skills such as learning a technical procedure should be easier to learn than broad ability domains such as verbal ability. Using Campbell's (1990) taxonomy of job performance behavior, Hellervik et al. (1992) offered several examples of behaviors that might be easy to develop (e.g., "write a grammatical sentence") and difficult to develop (e.g., "prepare a scientific treatise"; p. 840). They take a within-dimension approach rather than a between-dimension approach, emphasizing that the developability of a behavior or skill is determined by its complexity rather than the dimension to which it belongs. Brush and Licata (1983) provided a different framework for identifying learnable skills. They proposed that skills that primarily depend on cognitive processes, such as acquiring specific knowledge or following set procedures, are the easiest to develop, whereas the development of skills requiring interpersonal interaction or noncognitive elements (i.e., changes in attitudes, dispositions, or values) prove more challenging. Waters (1980) offered a somewhat more detailed model, distinguishing managerial skills according to the degree of behavioral specificity with which they are defined. He argued that practice skills and insight skills can be learned within a relatively short interval—a span of hours or days—whereas context skills and wisdom might take several weeks or months. Practice skills (e.g., active listening) are behaviorally specific (as AC dimensions are intended to be), whereas insight skills (e.g., "dealing with peers," p. 451) are considered behaviorally nonspecific. Waters took a fairly optimistic view of development, assuming that most skills can be developed in time, but Brush and Licata (1983) expected that some skills would display "low learnability" (p. 33).

Although the ideas proposed by Brush and Licata (1983), Hellervik et al. (1992), and Waters (1980) are clearly relevant to the question of dimension choice for DACs, none of these works presents empirical evidence in support of those ideas. Nor does it appear that any systematic evaluation of any of these theories has been conducted to date, either by the original authors or by others. The bulk of research reports regarding managerial skill development focuses on a single dimension or a cluster of related dimensions, and explicit comparisons of developability between dimensions are rare. However, some tangential evidence exists. For example, Norman (2003) assessed the effectiveness of a trust-building training program that included aspects of leadership and listening. She found that participants' subordinates reported seeing improvement in what she termed *scheduled behavior* (specific activities that occur at designated times in the course of the job, such as formal coaching) but not in *ongoing behavior* (relationship-oriented activities that can occur at any point, such as listening). This is consistent with Brush and

Licata's hypothesis that skills that involve following a method or procedure (such as running a scheduled coaching session) can be learned more quickly than can skills involving less structure and more variable human interaction.

PERCEPTIONS OF DEVELOPABILITY

A growing body of research indicates that objective evidence of developability may not be the only basis on which to determine whether development is likely to occur. Recent social psychological research regarding implicit theories has shown that individuals vary in their beliefs about the malleability or permanence of various attributes (e.g., intelligence, personality) and that these beliefs predict a number of behaviors (e.g., Dweck & Leggett, 1988), many of which are particularly relevant to development. For example, people who believe that intelligence is changeable are more likely to persist in challenging learning tasks than are those who hold an implicit theory that intelligence is fixed (Diener & Dweck, 1978, 1980). Similarly, Dunning (1995) found that the importance of traits and their perceived modifiability affect the degree to which people display self-assessment versus self-enhancement preferences for receiving feedback. People who perceived a trait as being changeable were more interested in receiving accurate feedback, but those who viewed the trait as being fixed had a stronger preference for favorable feedback. Implicit theories about developability appear to be domain specific; students' theories about the changeability of their academic interests predicted persistence in their chosen majors, but their theories about intelligence did not (Zuckerman, Gagne, & Nafshi, 2001). This finding suggests that people's beliefs about the developability of specific dimensions are likely to influence their development behavior relative to those dimensions.

This research is critically important for practitioners developing DAC programs, because it implies that development behavior in or following a DAC may depend greatly on the participants' individual beliefs about whether the dimensions assessed are developable. The findings described here suggest that people will be interested in attending a DAC, engaged in the process, and responsive to feedback when they believe that there is a real probability that they can develop as a result. Conversely, research indicates that when people do not believe that they can change with respect to a given competency and when they believe that their present level of ability is low, they are likely to avoid challenges and other activities that foster development (Dweck & Leggett, 1988).

This is not to say that perceptions of developability are more important than objective developability or that DAC designers should incorporate dimensions that are widely believed to be developable without regard for evidence about their actual developability. Some dimensions may prove, if not impossible to develop, at least very difficult or not appropriate for development via DAC methods. However, the DAC designer must also keep in mind that objective evidence of developability does not necessarily lead to perceived developability. Participants may not be aware of or influenced by research evidence showing that a skill can be developed. For example, despite many studies describing successful interventions to increase creativity (e.g., Basadur, Wakabayashi, & Takai, 1992; Roland, 1998), many people believe that creativity is an inherent, stable characteristic. Zuckerman et al. (2001) argued that the interaction of beliefs and evidence about developability is important; in other words, believing that dimensions can be developed is beneficial when they are in fact developable but not if they are stable or fixed. The best dimensions for a DAC, then, should be those that are relevant to job success, that can be shown to be developable, and that are seen as being developable by the participants.

CHOOSING DAC DIMENSIONS

In choosing dimensions for any AC, the practitioner's main task is to identify the set of dimensions that are relevant for the job in question and then determine which subset of those dimensions should be used for the center. It is possible that considerable overlap exists between the subset of dimensions that are most appropriate for ACs and the subset that is best for DACs, or it is possible that the overlap is slight. Designers who assume that the subsets are identical run the risk of investing in a costly, time-consuming process that may not produce the desired results. Further, identifying objectively developable dimensions alone may not be sufficient if they are not also perceived as being developable. Of course, development cannot be expected to occur on dimensions that are perceived as being developable but are not actually so; dimensions that are accurately perceived as being developable constitute a subset of the objectively developable dimensions. Because the research on implicit theories has not yet specifically examined managerial performance dimensions, it is not yet possible to say what proportion of developable dimensions are likely to fall into this subset.

Figure 2 illustrates the process for choosing DAC dimensions to maximize the opportunity for development:

1. Begin by identifying a set of job relevant dimensions.
2. Choose from that set the dimensions that have been shown to be amenable to development.
3. Choose from the resulting subset those dimensions that are perceived by most of the target population as being developable.

NONTRADITIONAL DIMENSIONS

In Figure 2, the best dimensions for DACs are described as a subset of the available job-relevant dimensions. This might suggest that DAC developers should focus on

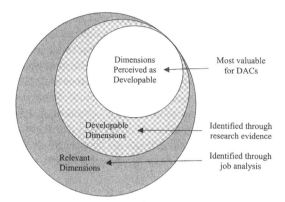

FIGURE 2   Identifying the most appropriate dimensions for DACs.

selecting the most developable dimensions from the set commonly used in traditional ACs. However, it is important to note that there may be dimensions that fall within the set of job-relevant dimensions but are not typically assessed by ACs. For selection or promotion ACs, the best dimensions are those that are most predictive of future potential. Often, this means that ACs focus on relatively stable characteristics (Howard & Bray, 1988) and basic abilities such as problem solving and interpersonal communication (Thornton & Rupp, 2005). If a person possesses reasonable ability in these areas, he or she can presumably be taught more specific skills later on the job. We have already argued that DACs may be better served by using developable, not stable, dimensions. Here, we note that DACs may be a highly appropriate way to address the specific skills eschewed by traditional ACs. Additionally, the rapid rate of change in today's workforce (Howard, 1995) often means that dimensions that would not have been important at the time that a manager was hired may become extremely important during the manager's tenure.

A concrete example is helpful here. Recent research makes a strong case for the importance of fair behavior on the part of managers (e.g., Colquitt, Conlon, Wessom, Porter, & Ng, 2001; Colquitt, Noe, & Jackson, 2002; Cropanzano, Rupp, Mohler, & Schminke, 2001; Liao & Rupp, 2005; Mossholder, Bennett, & Martin, 1998; Naumann & Bennett, 2000). There also exists evidence that fairness is a learnable, trainable skill (Cole & Latham, 1997; Skarlicki & Latham, 1996, 1997). An organization might wish to improve the overall level of fairness among its managers, but selecting new managers for their proficiency in fairness may seem impractical or even unfair, given the newness of this research and the fact that few managers will have received previous training in fairness. Fairness would be an unlikely candidate for inclusion in a traditional AC. However, a DAC might prove an ideal venue to introduce such a skill, explain its importance, assess participants' existing proficiency, and provide constructive feedback and practice. A similar argument could be made for cultural sensitivity, technology-mediated communication, and other specific but complex skills that might be relevant to a particular job but not appropriate for use in a selection AC. We encourage DAC developers to consider the entire set of job-relevant dimensions, including those that might be overlooked in ACs for selection purposes and to consider how DACs may be used to develop these less-traditional skills.

RECOMMENDATIONS FOR RESEARCH

The concept of developability of performance dimensions needs further explication. Our purpose in the present section is to propose a framework for future research in this area and to make practitioners aware of the gaps and issues that presently exist. A comprehensive analysis of the extent to which each performance dimension can be developed must include several aspects of development, including changeability, time required, and methods of change. Characteristics of the dimension itself should also be considered, such as complexity (Hellervik et al., 1992), specificity (Waters, 1980), and cognitive or interpersonal orientation (Brush & Licata, 1983). In addition, it is quite possible that various aspects of a dimension may develop at different rates. For example, both nonverbal communication and audience-appropriateness are elements of oral communication. It may be quite easy to develop nonverbal communication techniques such as eye contact and effective gestures, yet considerably more in-depth training may be required to learn how to gauge the appropriateness of one's communication for one's audience (cf. Hellervik et al., 1992; Waters, 1980). Future research is needed that explores the developability of the broad dimension classes and the individual behaviors of which they are composed. The top half of Table 2 presents a preliminary scaling of a few dimensions along such a continuum. The location of these initial dimensions is tentative, though suggested by previous research and experience (Brush & Licata, 1983; Hellervik et al., 1992; Waters, 1980). Systematic study over time is needed to confirm or refine the proposed scaling.

In addition to changeability, one must consider the element of time that is implied in the notion of developability (Waters, 1980). Some dimensions may be changed relatively quickly with little effort, whereas improvement in others may require considerable effort over an extended period of time. Knowing when development can be expected to take place is a critical issue for practitioners who must account for the effectiveness of their interventions. The element of time may also include consideration of maintenance of change and transfer to the work environment (cf. Baldwin & Ford, 1988).

A final consideration involves the methods most effective in improving performance for each dimension. A recent meta-analysis (Arthur, Bennett, et al., 2003) found that training methods may be differentially effective for different kinds of

TABLE 2
A Scale of Developability of Dimensions/Competencies
With Associated Development/Training Methods

	Nearly Impossible to Develop	Very Difficult to Develop	Difficult to Develop	Reasonable Possibility to Develop	Somewhat Easy to Develop
Dimensions/competencies	Motivation	Adaptability Conscientiousness	Interpersonal skills Leadership	Listening Problem-solving techniques Planning and organizing techniques	Nonverbal communication
Training methods		Long-term practice with coaching Extensive counseling	Counseling Education programs Long training programs Courses Mentoring Skill practice	Feedback alone Lecture Readings On-the-job experience with coaching	Participation in simulation alone Self-insight

Note. From *Assessment Centers in Human Resource Management*, p. 244, by G. C. Thornton and D. E. Rupp, 2005, Mahwah, NJ: Lawrence Erlbaum Associates, Inc. Copyright 2005 by Lawrence Erlbaum Associates, Inc. Reprinted with permission.

skills, but the authors noted that the reason for this is not yet clear. Systematic research is needed to identify the factors that influence the rate and degree of development for various dimensions, as is research that explores the types of interventions needed to develop various dimensions. For some dimensions, improvement may come with little more than the opportunity to participate in some activity that gives the participant self-insight, which can then readily result in behavioral change. Research findings suggest that AC participants can in fact gain such self-awareness, even before feedback is given (Schmitt, Ford, & Stults, 1986). By contrast, change in other dimensions may require extensive formal education or in-depth, lengthy, and individualized training. These elements can be incorporated into a long-term DAC program, such as the longitudinal DAC model proposed by Thornton and Rupp (2005), but would require substantial amounts of time, resources, and organizational buy-in. The lower half of Table 2 presents a preliminary scaling of intervention methods along the continuum of developability.

The multiple aspects of the extent to which various performance dimensions can be developed require further theoretical and empirical investigation. To create programs that effectively improve managerial competencies, DAC architects must thoroughly explore not only which dimensions (or aspects of each dimension) are most developable, but also which interventions and time frames are most appropriate for each. Past research has provided some insights into some of the answers such an investigation may yield.

For example, time and experience alone may be an effective developmental tool for some individuals and some dimensions but not necessarily for all. One of the most comprehensive studies of managerial development, the longitudinal Management Progress Study (Howard & Bray, 1988), found a general pattern of improvement in cognitive skills (defined as problem analysis and decision making) over time but a general decline in interpersonal skills. The data also suggest that development over time was at least partly a function of the ability level of the participants such that high-ability managers experienced performance gains over the first 8 years of assessment but that low-ability managers experienced performance losses. These findings imply that those who need to develop the most are not likely to develop over time in the natural course of experiential activities on the job. More research is needed to establish the characteristics of dimensions and individuals that make development most likely.

Other research offers information about specific types of interventions that have proven effective in managerial development. For example, interventions based on social learning theory (Bandura, 1997), in which effective behaviors are modeled for participants, show promise. In the arena of supervisory training, programs following principles of social learning theory (Goldstein & Sorcher, 1973) have shown positive results (Latham & Saari, 1979). These studies provide clues to promoting actual improvement in performance dimensions through DACs. Participants' skill development in a DAC may benefit from being provided with several guidelines or tools not common in traditional ACs. These include a conceptual model for handling the situations present in simulation exercises, clear step-by-step instructions on the actual behaviors that would be effective in handling each situation, and feedback on the effectiveness of initial behaviors followed by an opportunity to express similar behaviors in later simulation exercises.

RECOMMENDATIONS FOR PRACTICE

The need for information about dimension developability poses a quandary for practitioners seeking to develop DACs. Obtaining empirical evidence about the effectiveness of DACs in improving particular dimensions requires existing DACs from which such evidence can be collected. Until a substantial body of evidence develops concerning the effectiveness of DACs for developing various dimensions, practitioners must seek alternative bases for choosing dimensions to include in DACs. The best places to start include (a) consulting the existing research literature regarding the developability of individual dimensions using other training methods and (b) investigating participants' (and other subject matter experts') beliefs about developability. Our discussion of developable performance dimensions does suggest a number of general principles for the development and administration of DACs. These include retaining focus on development; carefully choosing dimensions; building participant self-efficacy; considering the effects of culture, differential development across individuals, and differences in DAC implementation on the DAC process; and evaluating effectiveness by measuring development.

Ensure That the Focus Remains on Development

Although quality assessment is necessary for providing accurate feedback, trade-offs between accuracy of assessment and developmental opportunity are likely to arise in the process of DAC development or administration. For example, providing feedback between exercises is beneficial from a developmental standpoint but problematic from an assessment standpoint. Using the same AC for both assessment and development can create numerous problems (for a detailed discussion of this issue, see Thornton & Rupp, 2005); nonetheless, this practice is common in organizations. Though we discourage the use of such hybrid centers, if they must be used, it is necessary to clearly identify one purpose—assessment or development—as primary and the other as secondary. Unlike traditional ACs, the primary deliverable of DACs is not overall assessment ratings or a set of recommendations but actual performance improvement. Thus, DAC developers must be aware both of measurement issues and of general principles of training and learning, and they must work to ensure that these issues are given sufficient emphasis.

Choose Dimensions Carefully

Though the DAC process is meant to provide opportunities for immediate development, not all dimensions in the program must be amenable to quick improvement. Consideration should be given to the time frame in which development is anticipated to occur. Development on some dimensions, such as oral communication, may occur during the DAC program, whereas improvement on other dimensions, such as planning and organizing, may appear after some weeks of practice. Positive change on some dimensions may require long periods of coaching or formal education to achieve. Even those dimensions that are perceived as being difficult to develop may be approached by providing feedback, setting goals, and suggesting training interventions. However, at least some of the dimensions should have the potential for development within the program or shortly after. Practitioners should keep these issues in mind both when choosing dimensions and when evaluating the effectiveness of the development program. The time horizon for development may also affect participants' (and management's) perceptions of developability. Long-term, difficult dimensions may be perceived as being undevelopable, which may lead to resistance. Therefore, special attention should be given to ensuring accurate conclusions about the developability of these dimensions and managing participants' efficacy for improving on them.

We warn readers not to conclude, given the arguments presented in this article, that nondevelopable traits are completely out of place in DAC programs. Although training on dimensions that cannot be developed may result in discouragement and learned helplessness, there may be utility in giving feedback on undevelopable traits to help participants learn to compensate for deficiencies in such areas. For example, a participant with a deficiency in a specific cognitive skill may not be able to improve himself or herself on that particular dimension. However, with appropriate feedback and coaching, this person may be able to learn ways around this limitation so that he or she can obtain equally effective results through other means. As mentioned, job relevance is the first criterion for including dimensions in the DAC program. If a nondevelopable dimension is highly relevant to a particular job but workarounds exist so that a lack of ability can be overcome, including the dimension in a DAC program may be beneficial for participants and the organization. Accurate feedback regarding a nondevelopable dimension may help people identify and implement such workarounds, improving performance overall even though the dimension per se is not improved. DAC developers should also think critically about how best to measure nondevelopable traits, in that traditional paper-and-pencil measures may be more appropriate than behavioral simulations in this case.

Build Participant Self-Efficacy

It is likely that many dimensions will prove to be both objectively developable and perceived as developable. However, situations may arise in which participants' perceptions do not match the objective evidence regarding developability (e.g., creativity). Thus, it is important to build efficacy for development by discussing the developability of the dimensions to ensure that participants share an optimistic view of the likelihood of performance improvement. Self-efficacy for learning is a critical component of development (McCauley & Hezlett, 2002); failure to generate efficacy or to include some dimensions that participants view as being improvable within a short time frame may generate responses of helplessness, negative attitudes, lack of motivation, and perceptions of lack of ability (Dweck, 1996). Orientations to DAC programs should address the absolute potential for development of each dimension as well as the anticipated time frame. This activity will contribute to resolution of misperceptions, development of realistic goals, and generation of increased motivation.

Consider the Effect of Culture

The culture in which the DAC is administered should be a crucial consideration in selecting the dimensions and exercises for the program. Differences in perception of importance, developability, and opportunities to improve performance outside of the DAC program are likely to affect participant perceptions of the usefulness of the process and influence the effort they exhibit. DACs should not be transported from one culture to another without examination of differences that may affect the effectiveness of the program.

Acknowledge Differential Development Across Individuals

Practitioners should be mindful of the role that individual differences may play in moderating development. For some participants, feedback alone may spur development on some dimensions, whereas little effect is seen for other people. A meta-analysis by Collins et al. (2003) found overall AC ratings to be significantly related to cognitive ability (.67), extraversion (.50), emotional stability (.35), openness (.25), and agreeableness (.17). Although the role of individual differences in changes in AC ratings has not been examined, the possibility of individuals' experiencing differential rates of change due to cognitive ability (cf. Hulin, Henry, & Noon, 1990) or personality characteristics is a potential factor that could affect DAC results.

Consider Variance in AC/DAC Practices

The principles proposed in this article and in future studies of DACs should be applied with the acknowledgement that many ACs in use serve multiple purposes. The consequences of decisions (such as dimensions to be included) have different effects for ACs with the purpose of development than for those with the purpose of selection. Even among development-only centers, purpose and implementation can vary widely: One DAC may be designed to prepare fast-track candidates for future promotions, whereas another may aim to correct current performance deficiencies. A single center may be unable to fulfill both objectives. Just as there is no typical AC (e.g., Thornton & Rupp, 2005), there is no typical DAC, especially given the newness of this area and the scarcity of empirical research. Only through future research and scholarly dialogue with practitioners can a general, consensus DAC model emerge. Regardless of design particulars, DAC practitioners must consider development issues (including dimension choice) and how the program can best be aligned with organizational goals.

Evaluate Effectiveness

As mentioned, the ultimate deliverable for DAC programs is performance improvement. Though DACs are popular in organizations, only a handful of studies thus far have evaluated the degree to which they are effective in producing such improvement (Engelbrecht & Fisher, 1995; Jones & Whitmore, 1995). Practitioners implementing DACs can make a substantial contribution to knowledge in this area by evaluating their DACs as they would any other training intervention (e.g., through pretest–posttest designs, control groups, consideration of multiple criteria; Kirkpatrick, 1967; Kraiger, Ford, & Salas, 1993). The recommendations in the present article suggest ways in which DAC designers can conduct strong tests of effectiveness by ruling out possible explanations for failure to develop (nondevelopable dimensions, low self-efficacy for learning). If well-designed DACs can be shown to be effective, then researchers can begin to investigate which design features are responsible for the effects and what boundary conditions may exist.

DACs appear to hold much promise as training and development interventions, yet a large number of questions must be answered before DACs can realize their full potential. Our purpose has been to call attention to one such question: How does one identify the most appropriate dimensions for a DAC? Borrowing performance models from traditional ACs does ensure that the dimensions used are job relevant, but such dimensions may not be the most amenable to development attempts. If the goal of DACs is to change behavior and improve performance, they will be most effective when they address important, job-relevant dimensions that can be developed given time and effort and that are understood to be developable by the participants. Failure to meet any of these three criteria will hinder the development of the participants and reduce the impact of the DAC. Much additional research is needed to identify which dimensions are most developable, how each is best developed, and in what time frames improvement can be expected. The present article provides a preliminary framework for researchers to explore these questions and for practitioners to make wise choices in designing DACs. It is our hope that researchers and practitioners will rise to the challenges presented here so that, in time, we will have a substantial body of evidence upon which dimension choice in future DACs can be based.

ACKNOWLEDGMENTS

The first three authors contributed equally to the manuscript. Alyssa Gibbons is supported by a National Science Foundation Graduate Research Fellowship. Any opinions, findings, conclusions, or recommendations expressed in this publication are those of the authors and do not necessarily reflect the views of the National Science Foundation.

REFERENCES

American Educational Research Association, American Psychological Association, & American Council on Measurement in Education. (1999). *Standards for educational and psychological tests.* Washington, DC: American Psychological Association.

Arthur, W., Jr., Bennett, W., Jr., Edens, P. S., & Bell, S. T. (2003). Effectiveness of training in organizations: A meta-analysis of design and evaluation features. *Journal of Applied Psychology, 88,* 234–245.

Arthur, W., Jr., Day, E. A., McNelly, T. L., & Edens, P. S. (2003). A meta-analysis of the criterion-related validity of assessment center dimensions. *Personnel Psychology, 56,* 125–154.

Arthur, W., Jr., Woehr, D. J., & Maldegen, R. (2000). Convergent and discriminant validity of assessment center dimensions: A conceptual and empirical reexamination of the assessment center construct-related validity paradox. *Journal of Management, 26,* 813–835.

Baldwin, T. T., & Ford, J. K. (1988). Transfer of training: A review and directions for future research. *Personnel Psychology, 41,* 63–105.

Ballantyne, I., & Povah, N. (2004). *Assessment and development centres* (2nd ed.). Aldershot, England: Gower.

Bandura, A. (1997). *Self-efficacy: The exercise of control.* New York: Freeman.

Basadur, M. S., Wakabayashi, M., & Takai, J. (1992). Training effects on the divergent thinking attitudes of Japanese managers. *International Journal of Intercultural Relations, 16,* 329–345.

Boehm, V. R. (1985). Using assessment centers for management development: Five applications. *Journal of Management Development, 4,* 40–53.

Borman, W. C., & Brush, D. H. (1993). More progress toward a taxonomy of managerial performance requirements. *Human Performance, 6,* 1–21.

Brush, D. H., & Licata, B. J. (1983). The impact of skill learnability on the effectiveness of managerial training and development. *Journal of Management, 9,* 27–39.

Buss, D. M., & Craik, K. H. (1983). The act frequency approach to personality. *Psychological Review, 90*(2), 105–126.

Byham, W. C. (1970). Assessment centers for spotting future managers. *Harvard Business Review, 48,* 150–160.

Campbell, J. P. (1990). Modeling the performance prediction problem in industrial and organizational psychology. In M. Dunnette & L. M. Hough (Eds.), *Handbook of industrial and organizational psychology* (2nd ed., Vol. 1, pp. 687–732). Palo Alto, CA: Consulting Psychologists Press.

Carrick, P., & Williams, R. (1999). Development centres—A review of assumptions. *Human Resource Management Journal, 9,* 77–91.

Chan, D. (1996). Criterion and construct validation of an assessment centre. *Journal of Occupational and Organizational Psychology, 69,* 167–181.

Chen, P. Y., Carsten, J., & Krauss, A. D. (2003). Job analysis: The basis for developing criteria for all human resources programs. In J. E. Edwards, J. C. Scott, & N. S. Raju (Eds.), *Human resources program-evaluation handbook* (pp. 27–48) Thousand Oaks, CA: Sage.

Cole, N. D., & Latham, G. P. (1997). Effects of training in procedural justice on perceptions of disciplinary fairness by unionized employees and disciplinary subject matter experts. *Journal of Applied Psychology, 82,* 699–705.

Collins, J. M., Schmidt, F. L., Sanchez-Ku, M., Thomas, L., McDaniel, M. A., & Le, H. (2003). Can basic individual differences shed light on the construct meaning of assessment center evaluations? *International Journal of Selection and Assessment, 11,* 17–29.

Colquitt, J. A., Conlon, D. E., Wesson, M. J., Porter, C. O. L. H., & Ng, K. Y. (2001). Justice at the millennium: A meta-analytic review of 25 years of organizational justice research. *Journal of Applied Psychology, 86,* 425–445.

Colquitt, J. A., Noe, R. A., & Jackson, C. L. (2002). Justice in teams: Antecedents and consequences of procedural justice climate. *Personnel Psychology, 55,* 83–109.

Constable, A. (1999, June). *Development centres.* Paper presented at the Human Resource Development Conference, London.

Cropanzano, R., Rupp, D. E., Mohler, C. J., & Schminke, M. (2001). Three roads to organizational justice. In J. Ferris (Ed.), *Research in personnel and human resource management* (Vol. 20, pp. 1–113). New York: JAI.

Diener, C. I., & Dweck, C. S. (1978). An analysis of learned helplessness: Continuous changes in performance, strategy, and achievement cognitions following failure. *Journal of Personality and Social Psychology, 36,* 451–462.

Diener, C. I., & Dweck, C. S. (1980). An analysis of learned helplessness: II. The processing of success. *Journal of Personality and Social Psychology, 39,* 940–952.

Dunning, D. (1995). Trait importance and modifiability as factors influencing self-assessment and self-enhancement motives. *Personality and Social Psychology Bulletin, 21,* 1297–1306.

Dweck, C. S. (1996). Capturing the dynamic nature of personality. *Journal of Research in Personality, 30,* 348–362.

Dweck, C. S., & Leggett, E. L. (1988). A social cognitive approach to motivation and personality. *Psychological Review, 95,* 256–273.

Engelbrecht, A. S., & Fischer, A. H. (1995). The managerial performance implications of a developmental assessment center process. *Human Relations, 48,* 387–404.

Gaugler, B. B., Bentson, C., & Pohley, K. (1990). *A survey of assessment center practices in organizations.* Unpublished manuscript.

Gaugler, B. B., Rosenthal, D. B., Thornton, G. C., III, & Bentson, C. (1987). Meta-analysis of assessment center validity. *Journal of Applied Psychology, 72,* 493–511.

Gaugler, B. B., & Thornton, G. C., III. (1989). Number of assessment center dimensions as a determinant of assessor accuracy. *Journal of Applied Psychology, 74,* 611–618.

Gibbons, A. M., & Rupp, D. E. (2004, April). *Developmental assessment centers as training tools for the aging workforce.* Paper presented at the 19th annual meeting of the Society for Industrial and Organizational Psychology, Chicago.

Goffin, R. D., Rothstein, M. G., & Johnston, N. G. (1996). Personality testing and the assessment center: Incremental validity for managerial selection. *Journal of Applied Psychology, 81,* 746–756.

Goldstein, A. P., & Sorcher, M. (1973). *Changing supervisor behavior.* New York: Pergamon Press.

Griffiths, P., & Goodge, P. (1994). Development centres: The third generation. *Personnel Management, 26*(6), 40–43.

Haaland, S., & Christiansen, N. D. (2002). Implications of trait-activation theory for evaluating the construct validity of assessment center ratings. *Personnel Psychology, 55,* 137–163.

Hardison, C. M., & Sackett, P. R. (2004, April). *Assessment center criterion-related validity: A meta-analytic update.* Paper presented at the 19th annual conference of the Society for Industrial and Organizational Psychology, Chicago.

Hellervik, L. W., Hazucha, J. F., & Schneider, R. J. (1992). Behavior change: Models, methods, and a review of evidence. In M. D. Dunnette & L. M. Hough (Eds.), *Handbook of industrial and organizational psychology* (2nd ed., Vol. 3, pp. 823–895). Palo Alto, CA: Consulting Psychologists Press.

Howard, A. (Ed.). (1995). *The changing nature of work.* San Francisco: Jossey-Bass.

Howard, A. (1997). A reassessment of assessment centers: Challenges for the 21st century. *Journal of Social Behavior and Personality, 12,* 13–52.

Howard, A., & Bray, D. W. (1988). *Managerial lives in transition: Advancing age and changing times.* New York: Guilford.

Hulin, C. L., Henry, R. A., & Noon, S. L. (1990). Adding a dimension: Time as a factor in the generalizability of predictive relationships. *Psychological Bulletin, 107,* 328–340.

Hunter, J. E., & Hunter, R. F. (1984). Validity and utility of alternative predictors of job performance. *Psychological Bulletin, 96,* 72–98.

Iles, P., & Forster, A. (1994). Developing organizations through collaborative development centers. *Organization Development Journal, 12,* 45–51.

International Task Force on Assessment Center Guidelines. (2000). Guidelines and ethical considerations for assessment center operations. *Public Personnel Management, 29,* 315–331.

Joiner, D. A. (2002). Assessment centers: What's new? *Public Personnel Management, 31,* 179–185.

Jones, R. G., & Whitmore, M. D. (1995). Evaluating developmental assessment centers as interventions. *Personnel Psychology, 48,* 377–388.

Joyce, L. W., Thayer, P. W., & Pond, S. B. (1994). Managerial functions: An alternative to traditional assessment center dimensions? *Personnel Psychology, 47,* 109–121.

Kirkpatrick, D. L. (1967). Evaluation of training. In R. L. Craig & L. R. Bittel (Eds.), *Training and development handbook* (pp. 87–112). New York: McGraw-Hill.

Kraiger, K., Ford, J. K., & Salas, E. (1993). Application of cognitive, skill-based, and affective theories of learning outcomes into new methods of training evaluation. *Journal of Applied Psychology, 78,* 311–328.

Kudisch, J. D., Avis, J. M., Fallon, J. D., Thibodeaux, H. F., Roberts, F. E., Rollier, T. J., et al. (2001, April). *A survey of assessment center practices in organizations worldwide: Maximizing innovation or business as usual?* Paper presented at the 16th annual conference for the Society of Industrial Organizational Psychology, San Diego, CA.

Kudisch, J. D., Ladd, R. T., & Dobbins, G. H. (1997). New evidence on the construct validity of diagnostic assessment centers: The findings may not be so troubling after all. *Journal of Social Behavior and Personality, 12,* 129–144.

Lance, C. E., Lambert, T. A., Gewin, A. G., Lievens, F., & Conway, J. M. (2004). Revised estimates of dimension and exercise variance components in assessment center postexercise dimension ratings. *Journal of Applied Psychology, 89,* 377–385.

Latham, G. P., & Saari, L. M. (1979). Application of social-learning theory to training supervisors through behavior modeling. *Journal of Applied Psychology, 64,* 239–246.

Lee, G. (2000). The state of the art in development centres. *Selection and Development Review, 16*(1), 10–14.

Lee, G., & Beard, D. (1994). *Development centres: Realizing the potential of your employees through assessment and development.* London: McGraw-Hill.

Liao, H., & Rupp, D. E. (2005). The impact of justice climate and justice orientation on work outcomes: A cross-level multifoci framework. *Journal of Applied Psychology, 90*, 242–256.

Lievens, F., & Conway, J. M. (2001). Dimension and exercise variance in assessment center scores: A large-scale evaluation of multitrait-multimethod studies. *Journal of Applied Psychology, 86*, 1202–1222.

McCauley, C. D., & Hezlett, S. A. (2002). Individual development in the workplace. In N. Anderson, D. S. Ones, H. Sinangil, & C. Viswesveran (Eds.), *Handbook of industrial, work, and organizational psychology: Vol. 1. Personnel psychology* (pp. 313–335). London: Sage.

McCormick, E. J. (1976). Job and task analysis. In M. D. Dunnette (Ed.), *Handbook of industrial and organizational psychology* (pp. 651–696). Chicago: Rand McNally.

McGeoch, J. A. (1929). The acquisition of skill. *Psychological Bulletin, 26*, 457–498.

Mossholder, K. W., Bennett, N., & Martin, C. L. (1998). A multilevel analysis of procedural justice context. *Journal of Organizational Behavior, 19*, 131–141.

Naumann, S. E., & Bennett, N. (2000). A case for procedural justice climate: Development and test of a multilevel model. *Academy of Management Journal, 43*, 881–889.

Norman, S. B. (2003). The effect of training managers to gain employee trust on employee work-related attitudes and emotional well-being (Doctoral dissertation, Stanford University, 2003). *Dissertation Abstracts International, 64*, 2428.

Robie, C., Osburn, H. G., Morris, M. A., Etchegaray, J. M., & Adams, K. A. (2000). Effects of the rating process on the construct validity of assessment center dimension evaluations. *Human Performance, 13*, 355–370.

Roland, R. S. (1998). Effects of training on divergent thinking attitudes of Turkish managers: A longitudinal study. In M. A. Rahim, R. T. Golembiewski, & C. C. Lundberg (Eds.), *Current topics in management* (Vol. 3, pp. 299–310). Greenwich, CT: JAI.

Rupp, D. E., & Thornton, G. C., III. (2003, October). *Consortium to study developmental assessment centers.* Paper presented at the 31st International Congress on Assessment Center Methods, Atlanta, GA.

Rupp, D. E., Thornton, G. C., III, & Gibbons, A. M. (2004, October). *Measuring change in a developmental assessment center: Evidence for construct validity.* Paper presented at the 32nd International Congress on Assessment Center Methods, Las Vegas, NV.

Sackett, P. R., & Dreher, G. F. (1982). Constructs and assessment center dimensions: Some troubling empirical findings. *Journal of Applied Psychology, 67*, 401–410.

Sackett, P. R., & Tuzinski, K. (2001). The role of dimensions and exercises in assessment center judgments. In M. London (Ed.), *How people evaluate others in organizations* (pp. 111–129). Mahwah, NJ: Lawrence Erlbaum Associates, Inc.

Salas, E., & Cannon-Bowers, J. A. (2001). The science of training: A decade of progress. *Annual Review of Psychology, 52*, 471–499.

Sanchez, J. I., & Levine, E. L. (2001). The analysis of work in the 20th and 21st centuries. In N. Anderson, D. S. Ones, H. K. Sinangil, & C. Viswesvaran (Eds.), *International handbook of work and organizational psychology* (pp. 71–89). Thousand Oaks, CA: Sage.

Schmidt, F. L., & Hunter, J. E. (1998). The validity and utility of selection methods in personnel psychology: Practical and theoretical implications of 85 years of research findings. *Psychological Bulletin, 124*, 262–274.

Schmidt, N., Ford, J. K., & Stults, D. M. (1986). Changes in self-perceived ability as a function of performance in an assessment centre. *Journal of Occupational Psychology, 59*, 327–335.

Schmitt, N., Noe, R. A., Meritt, R., & Fitzgerald, M. P. (1984). Validity of assessment center ratings for the prediction of performance ratings and school climate of school administrators. *Journal of Applied Psychology, 69*, 207–213.

Skarlicki, D. P., & Latham, G. P. (1996). Increasing citizenship behavior within a labor union: A test of organizational justice theory. *Journal of Applied Psychology, 81*, 161–169.

Skarlicki, D. P., & Latham, G. P. (1997). Leadership training in organizational justice to increase citizenship behavior within a labor union: A replication. *Personnel Psychology, 50,* 617–633.

Spychalski, A. C., Quiñones, M. A., Gaugler, B. B., & Pohley, K. (1997). A survey of assessment center practices in organizations in the United States. *Personnel Psychology, 50,* 71–90.

Tett, R. P., Guterman, H. A., Bleier, A., & Murphy, P. J. (2000). Development and content validation of a "hyperdimensional" taxonomy of managerial competence. *Human Performance, 13,* 205–251.

Thornton, G. C., III, & Byham, W. C. (1982). *Assessment centers and managerial performance.* New York: Academic Press.

Thornton, G. C., III, & Rogers, D. A. (2001, October). *Developmental assessment centers: Can we deliver the essential elements?* Paper presented at the 29th International Congress on Assessment Center Methods, Frankfurt, Germany.

Thornton, G. C., III, & Rupp, D. E. (2003). Simulations and assessment centers. In J. C. Thomas (Ed.) & M. Hersen (Series Ed.), *Comprehensive handbook of psychological assessment: Vol. 4. Industrial and organizational assessment* (pp. 319–344). Hoboken, NJ: Wiley.

Thornton, G. C., III, & Rupp, D. E. (2005). *Assessment centers in human resource management.* Mahwah, NJ: Lawrence Erlbaum Associates, Inc.

U.K. Industrial Society. (1996). *Assessment and development centres* (Managing Best Practice Series No. 29). London: Author.

Waters, J. A. (1980). Managerial skill development. *Academy of Management Review, 5,* 449–453.

Wexley, K. N., & Baldwin, T. T. (1986). Management development. *Journal of Management, 12,* 277–294.

Woehr, D. J., & Arthur, W., Jr. (2003). The construct-related validity of assessment center ratings: A review and meta-analysis of the role of methodological factors. *Journal of Management, 29,* 231–258.

Zuckerman, M., Gagne, M., & Nafshi, I. (2001). Pursuing academic interests: The role of implicit theories. *Journal of Applied Social Psychology, 31,* 2621–2631.

THE PSYCHOLOGIST-MANAGER JOURNAL, 2006, 9(2), 99–123

A Preliminary Investigation of Developable Dimensions

Alyssa Mitchell Gibbons and Deborah E. Rupp
Department of Psychology
University of Illinois at Urbana-Champaign

Lori A. Snyder
Department of Psychology
University of Oklahoma

A. Silke Holub and Sang Eun Woo
Department of Psychology
University of Illinois at Urbana-Champaign

This article poses the question, what do researchers know about the developability of the dimensions commonly used in assessment centers? A brief review of the training and development literature is used to explore empirical evidence for the developability of 16 common managerial performance dimensions. A survey of 139 managers is used to investigate participants' perceptions regarding the developability of the dimensions. Four nontraditional dimensions are proposed through constructs of interest in the recent research literature: fairness, cultural adaptability, emotion management, and readiness to develop. Survey results indicate that most of the nontraditional dimensions are perceived as being comparable to traditional dimensions in developability and importance.

Organizations are increasingly using developmental assessment centers (DACs) as a means of facilitating employees' professional development, particularly for complex skills such as leadership and interpersonal communication (Ballantyne & Povah, 2004; Kudisch et al., 2001; Spychalski, Quiñones, Gaugler, & Pohley, 1997). The assessment center method uses behavioral simulation exercises as a

Correspondence should be sent to Deborah E. Rupp, Department of Psychology and Institute of Labor and Industrial Relations, University of Illinois at Urbana-Champaign, 603 East Daniel Street, Champaign, IL 61820, E-mail: derupp@uiuc.edu

means of directly evaluating participants' behavior in realistic workplace scenarios (International Task Force on Assessment Center Guidelines, 2000). Traditional assessment centers (ACs) enjoy a strong reputation for validity when used to make selection or promotion decisions (e.g., Chan, 1996; Gaugler, Rosenthal, Thornton, & Bentson, 1987; Jansen & Stoop, 2001; Tziner, Ronen, & Hacohen, 1993), but much less is known about their effectiveness in developing employees. This distinction is critical because although the goal of traditional ACs is to predict future performance, the goal of DACs is to initiate behavior change, and the best means of attaining one goal may not be the best means to attain the other (Rupp, Snyder, Gibbons, & Thornton, this issue, p. 75; Thornton & Rupp, 2005). As a result, a number of researchers and practitioners (Carrick & Williams, 1999; Rupp, Snyder, et al., this issue; Thornton & Rogers, 2001; Thornton & Rupp, 2005) have called for rigorous research into the developmental aspects of DACs.

One urgent research need, as noted by Rupp, Snyder, and colleagues (this issue, p. 75), concerns the constructs, or behavioral dimensions, that are most appropriately measured and developed in DACs. Dimensions are sets of job-relevant behaviors that can be logically grouped together, such as planning or conflict management (Thornton & Byham, 1982).[1] Dimensions for an AC are typically chosen for their relevance to the target job and are based on job analysis (International Task Force on Assessment Center Guidelines, 2000). Many job-analytic methods are available to the practitioner developing an AC (e.g., Chen, Carsten, & Krauss, 2003; McCormick, 1976; Sanchez & Levine, 2001), and a substantial body of research has developed regarding the relevance and predictive validity of many commonly assessed dimensions (for a meta-analysis of this literature, see Arthur, Day, McNelly, & Edens, 2003). A number of resources are therefore available to guide the process of dimension choice for a traditional AC. Rupp, Snyder, and colleagues (this issue), however, argued that the dimensions used in DACs should be not only job relevant but also developable. If the goal of a DAC is to catalyze performance improvement on the dimensions, the dimensions chosen should be those on which a participant can reasonably expect to improve given time and effort.

The AC literature provides far less guidance about the developability of dimensions. The best test of whether a dimension is developable via DACs is to examine DACs featuring that dimension and to consider the amount of development that oc-

---

[1]Several researchers (e.g., Lance, Lambert, Gewin, Lievens, & Conway, 2004; Sackett & Dreher, 1982; Sackett & Tuzinski, 2001) have questioned the appropriateness of using dimensions at all, because it is difficult for assessors to distinguish between dimensions in the same exercise. Although some alternatives to dimensions have been proposed (e.g., managerial functions; Joyce, Thayer, & Pond, 1994), they have not been widely implemented in operational ACs (Lance et al., 2004). Most ACs and DACs continue to be designed around dimensions (Thornton & Rupp, 2005).

curs. However, such data have seldom been reported in the DAC literature. We identified over 30 recent research publications, technical reports, and practitioner articles focusing on DACs. Of these, only 14 described the dimensions used, and of those, only 1 reported outcome data regarding participants' development on the dimensions (Engelbrecht & Fischer, 1995; performance improved on six of eight dimensions measured). More research is clearly needed in this area, but such research requires DACs, and DACs must be based on some set of dimensions. How, in the meantime, are DAC developers to make informed decisions about which dimensions to include?

The purpose of the present article is to investigate the available evidence regarding the developability of dimensions commonly assessed in ACs. Although the DAC literature has not focused on developability, many other types of training interventions exist for managerial skills, and reports from these interventions may be useful for DAC developers. In taking a preliminary step in the development of a general multiorganizational DAC for midlevel managers (see Rupp, Gibbons, et al., this issue, p. 171), we identified 16 general dimensions most often considered important for this group (i.e., those most likely to emerge from job analyses across organizations), and we based them on models of managerial performance from the research literature, existing ACs, and human resource management consulting firms. This allowed us to limit our focus to a manageable number of dimensions while targeting those most likely to be of interest to practitioners developing DACs. We then reviewed literature in training and development in search of information about the developability of each dimension, with particular emphasis on studies that used methods similar to those used in DACs (e.g., role-playing, practice, feedback).

Following the recommendations of Rupp and colleagues (this issue, p. 171), we investigated managers' perceptions of the developability of the dimensions. Rupp and colleagues argued that though objective (i.e., empirically demonstrated) developability is a critical criterion for DAC dimensions, it is important to investigate participants' beliefs about the developability of the dimensions. Believing that a dimension is changeable does not necessarily make it so, but research in social and personality psychology suggests that the converse may be true: People who believe that a characteristic cannot be changed or developed are unlikely to pursue or persist in development efforts (Diener & Dweck, 1978, 1980; Dunning, 1995; Zuckerman, Gagne, & Nafshi, 2001). Information about perceived developability may be useful in guiding dimension choice or in designing other aspects of the DAC program. Dimensions that are widely perceived as being developable may attract participants to a DAC and encourage development efforts from them. If a dimension is important to the target job and if evidence suggests that it is objectively developable but not perceived to be so, the DAC staff may take extra pains to explain to participants that development is possible and hence build their self-efficacy.

IDENTIFICATION OF COMMON MANAGERIAL
PERFORMANCE DIMENSIONS

To identify commonly measured dimensions of managerial performance, we conducted an extensive literature search that included journal articles, conference papers, unpublished manuscripts, AC technical reports, O*NET, and performance models used by major human resource management consulting firms. Models used in operational ACs were included whenever possible, but models derived for other purposes and general managerial performance taxonomies (e.g., Tett, Guterman, Bleier, & Murphy, 2000) were also included to be reasonably representative of all skills needed by managers. Each dimension and its definition were entered into a database and identified by source. In all, 1,095 dimensions were identified from 65 sources.[2]

Many dimensions overlapped in terms of their general meaning, but the names applied to the dimensions varied widely across sources. For example, a dimension involving the ability to convince others to agree with one's ideas might be labeled *persuasiveness* by one source, *persuasion and sales ability* by another, and *influence* by a third. We therefore used a multistep procedure to group dimensions conceptually rather than simply by label. First, we used an automated query technique to identify dimensions that contained 1 of 110 conceptual keywords (e.g., *collaboration*) in any part of the dimension title or definition. Keywords were generated by two researchers, who identified words that appeared frequently in the database. In all, 1,004 dimensions (92% of the database) contained at least 1 of the 110 keywords used in the search. It was possible for a dimension to map to more than one keyword; in fact, this was frequently the case, resulting in over 2,500 dimension–keyword pairs. The automated process was then examined for misleading matches by two raters, who manually assessed each entry for a conceptual match between the keyword and the dimension title and definition. Raters agreed in their judgments of match or mismatch on 83.6% of the dimension–keyword pairs.

Three additional raters then reviewed the keywords for obvious linguistic similarity (e.g., *perseverance* and *persistence*) and collapsed them into 55 dimension categories. A panel of three subject matter experts with extensive research and consulting experience in the areas of traditional ACs, DACs, training, and career development then reviewed the list of keyword categories and identified those that could logically be collapsed or combined further. Subject matter expert ratings were in agreement 90% of the time. When a disagreement occurred, subject matter experts discussed the dimensions until consensus was reached.

The result was a list of 16 dimensions that appeared to be consistently identified as being critical for successful managerial performance. For convenience, the subject matter experts independently grouped the dimensions into four clusters based

---

[2]A bibliography of these sources is available from the first author upon request.

on conceptual similarity. The subject matter experts' agreement on the clustering of dimensions was above 90%. Again, disagreements were resolved through discussion. Based on the dimensions within each category, the clusters were labeled *problem solving, approach to work, relational skills,* and *communication* respectively (see Table 1). Definitions for the final set of dimensions were derived from the database. A team of researchers listed, reviewed, and then condensed the definitions associated with all entries in a dimension category. Because the dimensions were intended for eventual use in an operational DAC, definitions were written to be consistent with research-based recommendations and professional guidelines (International Task Force on Assessment Center Guidelines, 2000; Thornton & Rupp, 2005). That is, they were written in terms of observable behaviors and in enough detail that assessors could be expected to make distinctions among them. In addition, care was taken to ensure that dimensions were distinguished clearly enough that an individual could feasibly assess well on one dimension and poorly on another, even within the same cluster (Thornton & Byham, 1982). These definitions appear in Table 1.

DIMENSION DEVELOPABILITY
IN THE RESEARCH LITERATURE

The 16 dimensions identified appear to represent critical skills for managerial success across many situations, jobs, and industries. As such, they are likely candidates for inclusion in a traditional managerial AC. Our present concern, however, is whether and to what extent they are developable and thus appropriate for use in managerial DACs. Waters (1980) proposed a model in which he differentiated four types of skills in terms of their developability and behavioral specificity: practice skills, insight skills, context skills, and wisdom. Practice skills are behaviorally specific and can be learned quickly; insight skills can also be learned quickly but are more difficult to define. Both context skills and wisdom are more difficult to develop; the former are behaviorally specific whereas the latter is abstract. Though Waters did not provide extensive lists of skills in each category, he did provide examples, many of which correspond to the 16 potential DAC dimensions identified here. Oral presentation (an aspect of oral communication) is considered a practice skill, as are conflict management and active listening. Teamwork, several aspects of relationship and interpersonal skills, and creativity are all categorized as insight skills. According to Waters, all of these would be quite developable. By contrast, several aspects of leadership, such as motivating others and asserting authority, are considered context skills, which require more time to learn. From Waters's classification, it appears that some aspects of some dimensions may be easier to develop than others. Managing meetings, which is a component of planning and organizing, is counted as a practice skill, but goal setting and time management are both

TABLE 1
Common Performance Dimensions for Midlevel Managers

Cluster	Dimension	Definition
Problem solving	Problem solving	After gathering all pertinent information, identifies problems and uses analysis to perceive logical relationships among problems or issues; develops courses of action; makes timely and logical decisions; evaluates the outcomes of a problem solution.
	Information seeking	Gathers data; identifies and finds relevant and essential information needed to solve a problem; effectively analyzes and uses data and information.
	Creativity	Generates and recognizes imaginative solutions and innovations in work-related situations; questions traditional assumptions and goes beyond the status quo.
Approach to work	Planning and organizing	Establishes procedures to monitor tasks, activities, or responsibilities of self and subordinates to ensure accomplishment of specific objectives; determines priorities and allocates time and resources effectively; makes effective short- and long-term plans; sets and uses appropriate priorities; handles administrative detail.
	Adaptability	Remains effective by modifying behavioral style to adjust to new tasks, responsibilities, values, attitudes, or people; shows resilience in the face of constraints, frustrations, or adversity.
	Stress tolerance	Maintains composure and performance under pressure, opposition, tight time frames, and/or uncertainty; directs effort to constructive solutions while demonstrating resilience and the highest levels of professionalism.
	Conscientiousness	Works efficiently and consistently toward goals with concern for thoroughness; consistently meets deadlines and expectations; displays concentration, organization, and attention to detail; thinks carefully before acting.
	Motivation	Originates action rather than passively accepting or responding to events; demonstrates capacity for sustained effort over long periods until the desired objective is achieved or is no longer reasonably attainable; expresses a desire for advancement through self-development efforts.

(continued)

Category	Competency	Description
Communication	Oral communication	Expresses thoughts verbally and nonverbally in a clear, concise, and straightforward manner that is appropriate for the target audience whether in a group or individual situation.
	Written communication	Expresses ideas clearly and succinctly in writing, using appropriate grammatical form for both formal and informal documents; adjusts writing style, tone, and language as indicated by the needs of the audience.
	Listening	Actively attends to and conveys understanding of the comments and questions of others in both group and individual situations; hears, pays attention to, and determines important information and ideas presented through spoken words and sentences; performs active listening by asking questions when appropriate.
	Persuasiveness	Uses written or oral communication to obtain agreement or acceptance of an idea, plan, activity, or product; demonstrates keen insight of others' behavior and tailors own behavior to persuade or influence them; gains support and commitment from others.
Relational	Relationship/ interpersonal skills	Initiates and maintains effective relationships by presenting oneself to others in a positive manner, even in the face of conflict; responds to the needs, feelings, and opinions of others; uses relationships appropriately to accomplish personal or organizational goals.
	Leadership	Guides, directs, and motivates subordinates toward important and challenging work in line with their interests and abilities as well as the needs of the organization; gives regular, specific, and constructive feedback to subordinates in relation to their personal goals; commands attention and respect; promotes positive change by setting goals and priorities that are in line with the common vision of the organization.
	Teamwork	Works effectively with others by cooperating and contributing to the pursuit of team goals; communicates decisions, changes, and other relevant information to the team in a timely manner; develops supportive relationships with colleagues and creates a sense of team spirit.
	Conflict management/ resolution	Recognizes and openly addresses conflict appropriately; arrives at constructive solutions while maintaining positive working relationships.

Note. From *Assessment Centers in Human Resource Management*, pp. 79–80, by G. C. Thornton and D. E. Rupp, 2005, Mahwah, NJ: Lawrence Erlbaum Associates, Inc. Copyright 2005 by Lawrence Erlbaum Associates, Inc. Reprinted with permission.

considered context skills, which require more time to develop. Unfortunately, Waters did not present an empirical test of his model, and to our knowledge neither he nor any subsequent researchers have conducted such a test.

Although there is little research that compares the developability of different dimensions with one another, this does not mean that nothing is known or can be known about developing individual dimensions. The following sections explore evidence regarding non-DAC development interventions, as reported by researchers and practitioners across a variety of contexts. Though it is not possible within the scope of this article to provide an exhaustive review of the training and development literature, the research discussed illustrates the variety of approaches taken to the problem of developing individuals on specific dimensions. Our goals in this section are twofold: first, to determine whether evidence exists that the dimension can be developed at all and, second, to gain a sense of the methods and time frames associated with successful interventions for each dimension. For clarity, the dimensions are organized into the clusters described in the preceding sections.

Problem-Solving Cluster

Problem solving is a complex skill, so it is not surprising that interventions to develop dimensions in the problem-solving cluster often focus on a single aspect of the process. However, many of these focused interventions appear to be quite effective. For example, Clinton and Torrance (1986) targeted problem identification skills and were able to produce dramatic improvement in a 2-hr session by teaching a simple four-step method. Divergent thinking, a skill related to problem solving and creativity, was shown to be developable using multiple methods in multiple cultures. A group of Turkish managers improved in divergent thinking following a 1-day didactic computer-based training program (Roland, 1998), and Japanese managers developed similar skills after a 4-hr experiential learning program (Basadur, Wakabayashi, & Takai, 1992). Many development interventions for information seeking are similarly focused on specific skills, such as effective use of library resources. For example, Fisher, Reardon, and Burck (1976) used behavior modeling techniques in a brief videotape to teach students how to find information in a university career center. The researchers found that students who watched the video engaged in more frequent and more varied information-seeking behavior within the center than did students who completed a paper instructional module. Other interventions, however, targeted information seeking at a broader level. Santos-Gomez (1991) found that diagnostic decision makers used more efficient information search strategies (seeking less irrelevant information) when their initial training about the decisions used a case method or taxonomic method rather than an inductive method. This study suggests that programs designed to develop one dimension (in this case, knowledge) may have indirect influences on participants' development on other dimensions (information seeking).

Communication Cluster

Oral and written communication skills are often addressed as part of formal management education, but job-related interventions for these skills also exist. Rogers and Hildebrandt (1993) described a structured method in which they provided managers with feedback from subordinates and peers regarding the content of their written and oral communications. The authors offered anecdotal evidence that their approach was received favorably by managers, but they provided no outcome data. In an intervention designed to help managers gain their subordinates' trust, Norman (2003) reported that listening skills did not significantly improve as a result of the training but that managers who completed the training were later perceived as having improved in benevolence, which was associated with better listening. Although many prescriptive texts and programs for developing persuasion skills exist, often based on extensive psychological research into the processes of persuasion, the extent to which these training methods are effective in teaching persuasion is less clear. Tysoe (1982) found that the common role-reversal method of training (in which negotiation trainees are encouraged to argue first from the opposing position and then from their own) did not result in persuasive negotiations but that teaching trainees to restate the position of the other side did.

Relational Cluster

Many managers place a high priority on developing their interpersonal skills. In a self-directed development program (Anderson, 1984), improving "interactive style with others" (p. 22) was the most commonly identified development goal. Participants in this program were provided with guidance in assessing their own developmental needs and were then instructed in general principles of self-development. In follow-up interviews, a majority of the group indicated that it had made substantial progress toward its development goals and could document achievements relative to those goals.

Many of the specific skills in the relational cluster have a substantial empirical research base. For example, the work of Salas and colleagues (e.g., Salas, Fowlkes, Stout, Milanovich, & Prince, 1999) on crew resource management in aviation has consistently demonstrated significant improvements in teamwork knowledge and actual behavior following a behavior-based crew resource management course including lecture, behavior modeling, practice, and feedback components. Other researchers have investigated more specific factors that facilitate teamwork development. Brown and Latham (2002) found that providing trainees with a list of effective teamwork behaviors was helpful to participants but only when they were instructed to set specific behavioral goals. Conflict management training also comes in many forms; for example, Anderson, Schultz, and Staley (1987) presented data showing that training in argumentativeness has a beneficial effect on conflict management skills for those who tend to be nonassertive.

Many leadership development programs also exist, but leadership is defined broadly in these cases, as in Anderson's program (1984), in which managers were encouraged to consider many dimensions (interpersonal skills, planning and organizing, delegation, etc.) as elements of their overall leadership style and develop whichever they chose. Similarly, Kho (2001) described a global leadership development program that measured no specific competencies but encouraged managers to discuss the insights they gained from overseas assignments. Many of the behaviors encouraged in Norman's trust-building training program (2003), such as providing feedback to subordinates, can be categorized as leadership under the model used in the present article. Norman found that managers improved specifically with respect to providing positive recognition and coaching, but many of the studies that construe leadership broadly provide only broad-level results. This focus makes it difficult to determine the developability of the narrower definition of leadership used here, though Norman's results provide encouragement that at least some specific leadership behaviors can be successfully taught.

Approach to Work Cluster

Some of the dimensions in the approach to work cluster are well established within the training and development literature, but others are more controversial. Planning and organizing, or time management skills, appear to be easy to learn; Van Eerde (2003) found that participants in a 1-day time management seminar reported positive benefits 1 month following training. There is also evidence that adaptability can be developed: Kozlowski et al. (2001) found that success in a computer simulation training program was related to trainees' subsequent performance adaptability. Strategies for stress-management training include hardiness training, which teaches trainees positive coping strategies for managing their perceptions of stressful situations (Maddi, Khan, & Maddi, 1998), and emotional intelligence training, which teaches principles for understanding one's own emotions and the emotions of others (Slaski & Cartwright, 2003). Both of these types of training had beneficial effects on participants' experiences of strain as a result of workplace stress.

The other two dimensions in this cluster, motivation and conscientiousness, are often construed as personality traits or stable individual differences—precisely the sort of dimensions that might be unlikely to develop in a DAC program. However, emerging research evidence suggests that they can in fact be developed to at least some degree. Singleton (1978) found significant increases in motivation for student leaders who participated in a semester-long managerial motivation development course but not for a control group who had expressed interest but been unable to take the course. Singleton used a variety of methods to encourage motivation among his students, including behavior modeling, case studies, and experiential learning projects. Unfortunately, the combination of methods and the duration of the course make it difficult to determine precisely how motivation was increased, but the study provides evidence that motivation may not be entirely fixed. Similarly, Robins, Fraley, Roberts, and Trzesniewski (2001) conducted a longitudinal study of personality in which they found a systematic pattern of increasing conscientiousness in college-age students over the 4 years of their university education. Although a large difference exists between 4 years of formal education and a few days spent in a DAC, the evidence that conscientiousness is changeable raises intriguing possibilities, especially given the importance of this characteristic to organizations.

Summary of Literature Review

The results of our exploration indicate that though the training and development literature is certainly large, it is not entirely satisfactory as a basis for identifying dimensions suitable for DACs. Theoretical models, such as those proposed by Waters (1980), have seldom been investigated in a systematic way, and most studies of development focus either on training principles independent of content (e.g., Salas & Cannon-Bowers, 2001) or on a single intervention targeted to a specific dimension. Many examples of the latter exist; we were able to find examples of successful development for every dimension that we identified. It is tempting to conclude that all dimensions are developable and that the entire question of developability is irrelevant for DAC design. However, the evidence does not fully warrant such a conclusion.

The studies that we reviewed varied considerably in method, population, length, and dimension definitions, all of which may have had significant impacts on their results; but the difficulty of comparing such widely different studies makes these effects nearly impossible to discern. Further, evaluating the effectiveness of development programs is widely acknowledged as one of the greatest challenges in the area of training and development (e.g., Salas & Cannon-Bowers, 2001; Wexley & Baldwin, 1986). Many programs settle for anecdotal participant reaction criteria ("I believe I learned a great deal") rather than more rigorous measures of transfer of training and organizational utility (see Salas, Burke, Bowers, & Wilson, 2001). The research reviewed here used many different types of criteria as the basis for claiming a successful intervention. Reports of successful development interventions are also far more likely to be submitted and accepted for publication than are reports of failures. Descriptions of failed interventions are difficult to find, though it is hard to believe that such failures are uncommon (Salas & Cannon-Bowers, 2001). On a more encouraging note, it appears that all the dimensions that we considered have been developed to some extent by some means, suggesting that none are completely fixed. Further, DAC-like elements such as role-playing, practice, and feedback appear to be effective strategies for developing several dimensions—for example, teamwork (Salas et al., 1999) and information seeking (Fisher et al., 1976).

MANAGERS' PERCEPTIONS OF DEVELOPABILITY

Although knowledge regarding developability beliefs could be highly valuable for practitioners designing DACs, as discussed here, little research exists to date regarding beliefs about the types of dimensions that are likely to be observed in ACs. An exception is the work of Wrenn and Maurer (2004), who investigated undergraduates' beliefs about the developability of 29 abilities considered essential for learning and development. The researchers found that abilities such as oral presentation and oral communication were seen as being highly developable, whereas abilities such as objectivity and scholastic aptitude were seen as being less so. Many of the abilities discussed by Wrenn and Maurer are similar to the dimensions identified here, but their focus is on a different population (undergraduate students) and domain (learning tasks) than in the present study. As a result, we believed that it would be valuable to gather data directly regarding perceived developability from managers similar to those for whom the AC was being designed.

We developed a survey in which managers in several organizations were asked to indicate their beliefs regarding the developability of the 16 dimensions described here. To verify the appropriateness of the dimensions we had chosen, the survey assessed respondents' perceptions of the importance of the dimensions. Because our determination of the relative importance of each dimension was largely based on the frequency with which they were mentioned in the literature, it seemed conceivable that a particular dimension (e.g., completing paperwork) might be a common but insignificant aspect of many managerial jobs. Such a dimension is unlikely to be particularly useful in a DAC. This allowed us to compare the relative importance of each dimension, at least as perceived by job incumbents.

Rupp, Snyder, and colleagues (this issue, p. 75) noted that the traditional emphasis on predictive dimensions for ACs may leave some important dimensions overlooked. They noted that constructs such as fairness are increasingly shown to be important managerial skills but that such constructs are seldom included in selection ACs, though they may prove to be highly developable (cf. Rupp, Baldwin, & Bashshur, this issue, p. 145). We therefore included a set of exploratory, nontraditional dimensions in the survey, based on current research in industrial and organizational psychology and human resource management, to see whether managers would perceive these dimensions as being appropriate for DACs. All of these dimensions have been shown to be important for managerial success in at least some contexts, though little is known about their importance when compared to more traditional dimensions. The four nontraditional dimensions were fairness (cf.

TABLE 2
Nontraditional Dimensions and Their Definitions

Dimension	Definition
Fairness	Displays sensitivity to the needs, feelings, and viewpoints of others; expresses honesty, sincerity, and neutrality; delivers all agreed-upon outcomes as promised; treats others with courtesy, respect, and dignity; maintains a consistent standard of treatment for all employees; shares information with subordinates; provides proper evidence/explanation of actions taken; provides subordinates with the appropriate levels of choice over their situations; allows employees to express their opinions.
Cultural adaptability	Makes correct (isomorphic — making approximately the same judgment about the cause of a behavior as do the people of the host culture) attributions regarding the behavior of others; communicates in a culturally appropriate manner; is effective in social interaction; does not experience culture shock; handles disconfirmed expectations — does not come to hurried conclusions about the causes of behavior when hosts do not meet expectations; expresses appreciation and value for others' viewpoints, ideas, opinions, judgments, beliefs, and personalities even when they conflict with one's own.
Emotion management	Expresses positive emotions that may or may not be truly felt; suppresses negative emotions that may or may not be truly felt.
Readiness to develop	Seeks feedback about own job performance and suggestions for improvement; accepts feedback from others in nondefensive way; expresses interest in personal growth and improvement in job performance; seeks out and engages in activities to improve ones' knowledge, skills, abilities, and other job-related characteristics; exerts active efforts toward self-development for advancement; is open to and actively involved in learning.

Colquitt, Noe, & Jackson, 2002; Cropanzano, Rupp, Mohler, & Schminke, 2001; Liao & Rupp, 2005; Mossholder, Bennett, & Martin, 1998; Naumann & Bennett, 2000), cultural adaptability (Bhawuk, 2001; Landis & Bhagat, 1996), emotion management (or emotional labor; Hochschild, 1983; Morris & Feldman, 1996), and readiness to develop (Walter & Thornton, 2004). Definitions for each of these dimensions appear in Table 2.

METHOD

Participants

Participants were 139 managers across the United States. We recruited the managers through personal contacts, and they represented a variety of industries, including food service, grocery, accounting, and retail. The sample was 52.5% female, and 15.5% reported belonging to a racial or ethnic minority group. The average age of the respondents was 37.13 years; their average tenure in the current job was 15.64 years; and their average time in the workforce was 20.93 years.

Procedure

The survey contained definitions for the 16 common managerial dimensions and the 4 nontraditional dimensions (see Tables 1 and 2). Respondents were asked to read each definition carefully rather than use their own interpretation of the terms. Then, pulling from classic job analytic techniques (Gael, 1988), we asked respondents to indicate their agreement with the following five statements with respect to each dimension:

1. It is important that managers possess this skill.
2. Managers need this skill for their future careers.
3. Successful managers use this skill on a regular basis.
4. This skill is needed to avoid negative consequences.
5. This skill can be learned/developed with training.

Agreement was indicated on a 5-point Likert scale ranging from 1 (*strongly disagree*), 2 (*disagree*), 3 (*neither disagree nor agree*), 4 (*agree*), to 5 (*strongly agree*). Each participant rated all five statements for each of the 20 definitions. Participants were also asked to complete a brief demographic questionnaire at the end of the survey, including questions about their current job and managerial experience.

RESULTS

Importance and Development Indexes

Responses to the first four of the five statements (importance, regular use, avoidance of negative consequences, and importance for future careers) were averaged to create a general importance index and measure of the degree to which the respondent considered the dimension important. The fifth item (learning or developing the dimension with training) was analyzed separately as a development index, indicating the degree to which the respondent believed that the dimension was amenable to development. Average interitem correlations (averaged across dimensions) can be seen in Table 3. These correlations generally support the grouping of items as described earlier; correlations among the first four items are moderately high (.47–.68), and the correlations of all other items with the fifth item are considerably lower (.26–.40). Mean importance and development index scores for all dimensions appear in Table 4.

TABLE 3
Average Interitem Correlations Among Survey Items

Item	1	2	3	4
1. It is important that managers possess this skill.				
2. Managers need this skill for their future careers.	.68			
3. Successful managers use this skill on a regular basis.	.53	.54		
4. This skill is needed to avoid negative consequences.	.47	.49	.48	
5. This skill can be learned/developed with training.	.26	.24	.29	.40

Importance

All dimensions had mean importance indexes above the scale's neutral point (3.0), confirming that respondents generally considered all the dimensions to be at least somewhat important. A series of one-sample t tests indicated that the difference from the neutral point was significant for all dimensions, using the Bonferroni correction for multiple comparisons (critical $\alpha = .002$). Leadership (4.54) was identified as the most important dimension, closely followed by planning and organizing, problem solving, teamwork, and conflict resolution (all = 4.47). Creativity (3.61) and emotion management (3.60) received the lowest importance indexes, though both were still described as being somewhat important.

No dimension was found to be significantly different from the dimensions immediately preceding or succeeding it in rank order of importance (based on the scores). However, dimensions at the upper end of the importance rankings were significantly different from those at the lower end. The dimensions can be grouped into slightly overlapping clusters, as represented in Figure 1. Dimensions within the same circle are not significantly different from each other; all other differences are statistically significant ($p \leq .003$, using the Bonferroni correction). Dimensions are shown in descending order by score.

Though agreement was reasonably high for all dimensions, somewhat greater diversity of opinion appeared for dimensions with lower importance ratings: The standard deviations for creativity and emotion management were 0.69 and 0.83 respectively, whereas the average standard deviation for importance indexes was 0.59 and the standard deviation for leadership only 0.46.

Development

Again, most dimensions received ratings significantly above the neutral point for perceived developability (one-sample t tests; critical $\alpha = .002$, using the Bonferroni correction for multiple comparisons). The only exceptions were creativity, with a development index of 2.96 ($p > .05$), and motivation, with a development index of 3.17 ($p > .002$). Written communication (4.09), planning and organizing

TABLE 4
Importance and Developability Scores

Cluster	Dimension	Importance Index		Development Index	
		M	SD	M	SD
Problem solving	Creativity	3.61	0.69	2.96	0.95
	Information seeking	4.23	0.57	4.01	0.72
	Problem solving	4.47	0.49	3.89	0.75
Approach to work	Adaptability	4.41	0.52	3.54	0.88
	Conscientiousness	4.33	0.26	3.51	1.03
	Motivation	4.14	0.50	3.17	0.97
	Stress management	4.29	0.12	3.62	1.00
	Planning and organizing	4.47	0.21	4.03	0.78
Relational	Relationship/interpersonal skills	4.21	0.23	3.60	0.83
	Teamwork	4.47	0.25	4.02	0.73
	Leadership	4.54	0.46	3.83	0.95
	Conflict management/resolution	4.47	0.19	3.97	0.77
Communication	Oral communication	4.44	0.37	3.99	0.75
	Written communication	4.06	0.30	4.09	0.70
	Listening	4.37	0.16	3.86	0.87
	Persuasiveness	3.83	0.46	3.43	0.87
Experimental	Cultural adaptability	4.28	0.30	3.55	0.87
	Emotion management	3.60	0.21	3.37	0.88
	Fairness	4.41	0.25	3.58	0.98
	Readiness to develop	4.07	0.34	3.51	0.92

(4.03), teamwork (4.02), and information seeking (4.01) received the highest development scores, indicating that respondents believed these skills could be developed with appropriate training. Figure 2 shows the rank ordering of dimensions by perceived developability, with dimensions that were not significantly different from one another shown within the same circle. There was less agreement among respondents in rating developability than in rating importance; the average standard deviation for the development index was 0.86. Thus, low development indexes may indicate diversity of opinion regarding the developability of a dimension rather than a shared perception that the dimension is difficult to develop.

Nontraditional Dimensions

The four nontraditional dimensions (cultural adaptability, emotion management, fairness, and readiness to develop) received importance ratings comparable to those of the traditional dimensions. Of the four, fairness was seen as being the most important ($M = 4.41$, $SD = 0.60$), followed by cultural adaptability ($M = 4.28$, $SD = 0.49$), readiness to develop ($M = 4.07$, $SD = 0.67$), and emotion management ($M =$

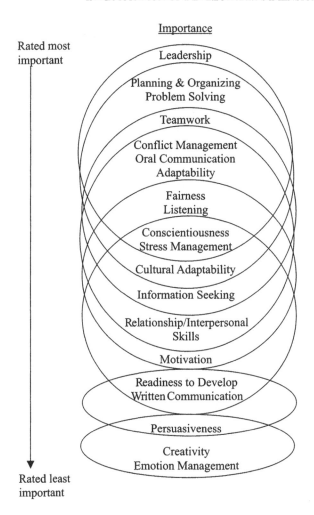

FIGURE 1   Managers' perceptions of importance. Dimensions within the same circle are not significantly different from one another (critical α =.002, using the Bonferroni correction for multiple comparisons).

3.60, SD = 0.83). Fairness was rated the eighth most important dimension overall, higher than a number of traditional managerial dimensions, such as motivation and information seeking. Though emotion management was rated the least important dimension overall, it still scored above the neutral point, indicating that respondents did not consider it unimportant. In addition, all of the nontraditional dimensions were seen as being at least moderately developable. Fairness was seen as being the most developable of these dimensions (M = 3.58, SD = 0.98), closely

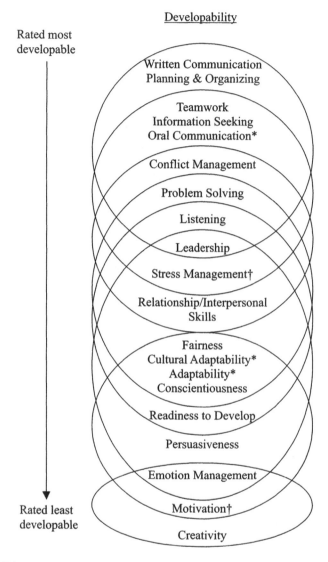

Developability

Rated most
developable

Written Communication
Planning & Organizing

Teamwork
Information Seeking
Oral Communication*

Conflict Management

Problem Solving

Listening

Leadership

Stress Management†

Relationship/Interpersonal
Skills

Fairness
Cultural Adaptability*
Adaptability*
Conscientiousness

Readiness to Develop

Persuasiveness

Emotion Management

Rated least
developable

Motivation†

Creativity

FIGURE 2   Managers' perceptions of developability. Dimensions within the same circle are
not significantly different from one another (critical $\alpha = .002$, using the Bonferroni correction
for multiple comparisons). Asterisks (*) denote that cultural adaptability and adaptability were
not significantly different from oral communication. Daggers (†) denote that motivation was
not significantly different from stress management.

followed by cultural adaptability ($M = 3.55$, $SD = 0.87$), readiness to develop ($M = 3.51$, $SD = 0.92$), and emotion management ($M = 3.37$, $SD = 0.88$). Although none of the nontraditional dimensions was among the top-ten developable dimensions, they remain comparable to some traditional dimensions, such as persuasiveness ($M = 3.43$, $SD = 0.87$) and motivation ($M = 3.17$, $SD = 0.97$). Overall, the nontraditional dimensions appear to have been perceived by the job incumbents as being similar to more traditional dimensions in terms of relevance and potential for development.

DISCUSSION

The purpose of the present study was to conduct a preliminary exploration of the objective (i.e., empirically demonstrated) and perceived developability of the dimensions likely to be used in managerial DACs. Such an investigation must necessarily be merely preliminary: A thorough evaluation of the developability of dimensions in DACs requires systematic research conducted in DACs. However, such DACs must be based on some set of dimensions. The present study suggests that until a more extensive literature regarding developability exists, DAC developers can make informed decisions about dimension choice by considering objective evidence in the training and development literature and by investigating beliefs about developability in the population of likely participants.

We reviewed the available research literature regarding the effectiveness of training and development interventions for 16 commonly assessed dimensions of managerial performance. Unfortunately, investigations of relative developability were few and far between; most studies focused on developing only a single skill. Definitions of success in development varied widely, as did the time intervals over which development was measured, making it difficult to form specific expectations about how much and how quickly development might occur. Despite these limitations, our review of the literature suggests that few dimensions are entirely undevelopable and that differences in developability are likely. Some skills appeared to improve quite quickly, at least within a limited context, such as Fisher et al.'s study (1976) of information seeking behavior. Van Eerde (2003) found that a simple 1-day intervention produced lasting improvement in time management skills. Other dimensions, such as motivation, appeared only in studies describing sustained, long-term interventions (Singleton, 1978).

Many parallels appear between the literature review and our survey of managers' beliefs about developability. Again, nearly all dimensions were believed to be at least somewhat developable. Planning and organizing, which was successfully developed in a brief period by Van Eerde (2003), was considered to be one of the most developable dimensions, but motivation was among those considered least developable (cf. Singleton, 1978). However, the objective and subjective evidence did not always agree. Although Basadur et al. (1992) and Roland (1998) found improvements in creativity following relatively short, simple interventions, managers considered creativity to be the least developable of the 20 dimensions included in the survey. This finding underscores the argument that both objective and subjective information about developability should be considered in designing a DAC (Rupp, Snyder, et al., this issue, p. 75; Zuckerman et al., 2001). If creativity is to be included in a DAC program, the DAC designers should consider how they might convey to participants that the dimension is in fact developable and that their development efforts will pay off. Conversely, it is unlikely that participants will see substantial improvement in conscientiousness immediately following a DAC, even though most managers believed it to be moderately developable. DAC designers in that case might be well advised to help participants set realistic expectations, to avoid disappointment and loss of self-efficacy.

Another notable finding was that our four nontraditional dimensions, selected not on the basis of job analysis but on the basis of current trends in the research literature, were nevertheless perceived by managers as being comparable to the more traditional dimensions in terms of developability and importance. Though emotion management was among the least important and least developable dimensions, fairness and cultural adaptability were in the middle of the rankings on both scales, with readiness to develop not far below. Managers generally indicated that these dimensions would be perceived as being appropriate in a DAC. This finding supports the argument made by Rupp, Snyder, et al. (this issue) that DACs may be useful venues to train skills that might not be considered for a selection AC.

Study Limitations

The study presented here is subject to a number of limitations that should be considered carefully in interpreting its results. First, the set of dimensions that we considered is by no means a complete performance model for all managerial jobs, nor does it represent a complete list of dimensions that might be considered suitable for DACs. We sought to use a systematic process to identify the dimensions most likely to be of interest to the readers of this article and to the participants in our DAC (cf. Rupp, Gibbons, et al., this issue, p. 171); however, many steps in the process required subjective judgment, and other researchers might reach different conclusions. Similarly, although we sought to obtain a broad and varied sample of managers, our participants are not necessarily representative of all organizations or industries. Different industries are likely to place different emphases on particular dimensions. For example, manufacturing organizations, which were not represented in our sample, might value dimensions such as creativity more highly than did the more service-oriented participants in the present study.[3] We stress that the

---

[3]We thank an anonymous reviewer for suggesting this example.

design of any AC or DAC should be based as far as possible on a job analysis conducted specifically for the target position.

Second, the literature review presented here is illustrative, not exhaustive. The training and development literature is vast, and the dimensions that we examined go by a number of different names. This factor made it difficult to be sure that we had identified every potentially relevant article, and it is likely that we missed some. However, our purpose was not to conduct a definitive review but rather to illustrate the types of information about the developability of individual dimensions that might be obtained from the research literature. Our primary conclusions appear justified on the basis of our search—namely, that each of our dimensions has been successfully developed by someone at some point and that few studies provide information comparing the developability of dimensions or identifying the appropriate time frame for development.

Third, our survey considered managers' perceptions of the developability of the dimensions, and one might question whether other experts, such as psychologists studying human abilities, would make similar judgments. Although the perceptions of psychologists or even experienced professional trainers might contribute additional valuable information to our understanding of developability, our concern was with the perceptions of potential DAC participants because their beliefs contribute to the face validity of the DAC process (Maurer, Weiss, & Barbeite, 2003) and may directly affect development-related behaviors, such as reception to feedback and persistence in developmental activities (e.g., Dunning, 1995; Dweck, 1996; Zuckerman et al., 2001). Further, the managers who participated in this study had on average more than 15 years of experience in management, many in positions or industries (e.g., grocery, retail) in which they would likely have been responsible for on-the-job training and development of subordinates. They did not necessarily have access to the same systematic body of knowledge that might be expected of industrial–organizational practitioners, but they did have a substantial amount of practical experience that should not be entirely discounted.

Another limitation with respect to perceptions of developability is that the existing research in this area focused on the individual level of analysis, but we examined perceptions at the group level. It seems clear that an individual's development behavior can best be predicted from his or her own beliefs about developability and that there is considerable variability in these beliefs for many important human attributes (Dweck & Leggett, 1988). The implication for DACs is that each participant will exert effort to develop those dimensions that he or she believes are developable and that individuals' different beliefs will lead them to respond to the DAC in different ways. However, DACs must be created for groups, not individuals, so a general knowledge regarding beliefs about developability in the target population is likely to benefit the DAC designer. If a dimension is widely believed to be stable and identified in the job analysis as being only moderately important, the designer may choose to exclude it from the DAC in favor of a dimension of similar importance that participants are more likely to see as being developable (and are therefore more likely to develop). If a critical dimension is viewed as being fixed by many participants, the designer who is aware of this perception can work to overcome it before or during the DAC, perhaps by providing information regarding previous successful interventions or individuals who have developed with respect to the dimension.

Most important, this study lays the groundwork for future research on the effectiveness of DACs. It illustrates arguments for considering objective and perceived developability in addition to job relevance when choosing dimensions for DACs. For 16 common managerial performance dimensions, it summarizes existing research evidence related to objective developability that, to our knowledge, has not previously been collected in one place. It also presents new evidence about the perceived developability of those dimensions, an issue that has important implications for the expected success of DACs and development interventions in general. Though much research is needed before we can establish a comprehensive model of developability in DACs, our findings offer a necessary first step in exploring developability and, by extension, best practices for DAC development.

ACKNOWLEDGMENTS

Alyssa Gibbons is supported by a National Science Foundation Graduate Research Fellowship. Any opinions, findings, conclusions, or recommendations expressed in this publication are those of the authors and do not necessarily reflect the views of the National Science Foundation.

The first, second, and third author contributed equally to this study. Portions of this article were presented at the 63rd annual meeting of the Academy of Management, Seattle, Washington.

We thank Kristin Konie and Tonya Runnels for their assistance with this project.

REFERENCES

Anderson, J. G. (1984). When leaders develop themselves. *Training and Development Journal, 38*(6), 18–22.

Anderson, J., Schultz, B., & Staley, C. C. (1987). Training in argumentativeness: New hope for nonassertive women. *Women's Studies in Communication, 10*(2), 58–66.

Arthur, W., Jr., Day, E. A., McNelly, T. L., & Edens, P. S. (2003). A meta-analysis of the criterion-related validity of assessment center dimensions. *Personnel Psychology, 56,* 125–154.

Ballantyne, I., & Povah, N. (2004). *Assessment and development centres* (2nd ed.). Aldershot, England: Gower.

Basadur, M. S., Wakabayashi, M., & Takai, J. (1992). Training effects on the divergent thinking attitudes of Japanese managers. *International Journal of Intercultural Relations, 16*, 329–345.

Bhawuk, D. (2001). Evolution of culture assimilators: Toward theory-based assimilators. *International Journal of Intercultural Relations, 25*, 141–163.

Brown, T. C., & Latham, G. P. (2002). The effects of behavioural outcome goals, learning goals, and urging people to do their best on an individual's teamwork behaviour in a group problem-solving task. *Canadian Journal of Behavioural Science, 34*, 276–285.

Carrick, P., & Williams, R. (1999). Development centres—A review of assumptions. *Human Resource Management Journal, 9*(2), 77–92.

Chan, D. (1996). Criterion and construct validation of an assessment centre. *Journal of Occupational and Organizational Psychology, 69*, 167–181.

Chen, P. Y., Carsten, J., & Krauss, A. D. (2003). Job analysis: The basis for developing criteria for all human resources programs. In J. E. Edwards, J. C. Scott, & N. S. Raju (Eds.), *Human resources program-evaluation handbook* (pp. 27–48). Thousand Oaks, CA: Sage.

Clinton, B. J., & Torrance, E. P. (1986). SEAM: A training program for developing problem identification skills. *Journal of Creative Behavior, 20*(2), 77–80.

Colquitt, J. A., Noe, R. A., & Jackson, C. L. (2002). Justice in teams: Antecedents and consequences of procedural justice climate. *Personnel Psychology, 55*, 83–109.

Cropanzano, R., Rupp, D. E., Mohler, C. J., & Schminke, M. (2001). Three roads to organizational justice. In J. Ferris (Ed.), *Research in personnel and human resource management* (Vol. 20, pp. 1–113). New York: JAI.

Diener, C. I., & Dweck, C. S. (1978). An analysis of learned helplessness: Continuous changes in performance, strategy, and achievement cognitions following failure. *Journal of Personality and Social Psychology, 36*, 451–462.

Diener, C. I., & Dweck, C. S. (1980). An analysis of learned helplessness: II. The processing of success. *Journal of Personality and Social Psychology, 39*, 940–952.

Dunning, D. (1995). Trait importance and modifiability as factors influencing self-assessment and self-enhancement motives. *Personality and Social Psychology Bulletin, 21*, 1297–1306.

Dweck, C. S. (1996). Capturing the dynamic nature of personality. *Journal of Research in Personality, 30*, 348–362.

Dweck, C. S., & Leggett, E. L. (1988). A social-cognitive approach to motivation and personality. *Psychological Review, 95*, 256–273.

Engelbrecht, A. S., & Fischer, A. H. (1995). The managerial performance implications of a developmental assessment center process. *Human Relations, 48*, 387–404.

Fisher, T. J., Reardon, R. C., & Burck, H. D. (1976). Increasing information-seeking behavior with a model-reinforced videotape. *Journal of Counseling Psychology, 23*, 234–238.

Gael, S. (Ed.). (1988). *Job analysis handbook for business, industry, and government*. New York: Wiley.

Gaugler, B. B., Rosenthal, D. B., Thornton, G. C., III, & Bentson, C. (1987). Meta-analysis of assessment center validity. *Journal of Applied Psychology, 72*, 493–511.

Hochschild, A. R. (1983). *The managed heart*. Berkeley: University of California Press.

International Task Force on Assessment Center Guidelines. (2000). Guidelines and ethical considerations for assessment center operations. *Public Personnel Management, 29*, 315–331.

Jansen, P. G. W., & Stoop, B. A. M. (2001). The dynamics of assessment center validity: Results of a 7-year study. *Journal of Applied Psychology, 86*, 741–753.

Joyce, L. W., Thayer, P. W., & Pond, S. B. (1994). Managerial functions: An alternative to traditional assessment center dimensions? *Personnel Psychology, 47*, 109–121.

Kho, E. C. (2001). An evaluation study of the effectiveness of a United States–based global leadership development program (Doctoral dissertation, California School of Professional Psychology, 2001). *Dissertation Abstracts International, 62*, 1120.

Kozlowski, S. W. J., Gully, S. M., Brown, K. G., Salas, E., Smith, E. M., & Nason, E. R. (2001). Effects of training goals and goal orientation traits on multidimensional training outcomes and performance adaptability. *Organizational Behavior and Human Decision Processes, 85*, 1–31.

Kudisch, J. D., Avis, J. M., Fallon, J. D., Thibodeaux, H. F., Roberts, F. E., Rollier, T. J., et al. (2001, April). *A survey of assessment center practices in organizations worldwide: Maximizing innovation or business as usual?* Paper presented at the 16th annual conference for the Society for Industrial Organizational Psychology, San Diego, CA.

Lance, C. E., Lambert, T. A., Gewin, A. G., Lievens, F., & Conway, J. M. (2004). Revised estimates of dimension and exercise variance components in assessment center postexercise dimension ratings. *Journal of Applied Psychology, 89*, 377–385.

Landis, D., & Bhagat, R. S. (1996). *Handbook of intercultural training* (2nd ed.). Thousand Oaks, CA: Sage.

Liao, H., & Rupp, D. E. (2005). The impact of justice climate and justice orientation on work outcomes: A cross-level multifoci framework. *Journal of Applied Psychology, 90*, 242–256.

Maddi, S. R., Khan, S., & Maddi, K. L. (1998). The effectiveness of hardiness training. *Consulting Psychology Journal: Practice and Research, 50*, 78–86.

Maurer, T. J., Weiss, E. M., & Barbeite, F. G. (2003). A model of involvement in work-related learning and development activity: The effects of individual, situational, motivational, and age variables. *Journal of Applied Psychology, 88*, 707–724.

McCormick, E. J. (1976). Job and task analysis. In M. D. Dunnette (Ed.), *Handbook of industrial and organizational psychology* (pp. 651–696). Chicago: Rand McNally.

Morris, J. A., & Feldman, D. C. (1996). The dimensions, antecedents and consequences of emotional labor. *Academy of Management Review, 21*, 986–1010.

Mossholder, K. W., Bennett, N., & Martin, C. L. (1998). A multilevel analysis of procedural justice context. *Journal of Organizational Behavior, 19*, 131–141.

Naumann, S. E., & Bennett, N. (2000). A case for procedural justice climate: Development and test of a multilevel model. *Academy of Management Journal, 43*, 881–889.

Norman, S. B. (2003). The effect of training managers to gain employee trust on employee work-related attitudes and emotional well-being (Doctoral dissertation, Stanford University, 2003). *Dissertation Abstracts International, 64*, 2428.

Robins, R. W., Fraley, R. C., Roberts, B. W., & Trzesniewski, K. H. (2001). A longitudinal study of personality change in young adulthood. *Journal of Personality, 69*, 617–640.

Rogers, P. S., & Hildebrandt, H. W. (1993). Competing values instruments for analyzing written and spoken management messages. *Human Resource Management, 32*, 121–142.

Roland, R. S. (1998). Effects of training on divergent thinking attitudes of Turkish managers: A longitudinal study. In M. A. Rahim, R. T. Golembiewski, & C. C. Lundberg (Eds), *Current topics in management* (Vol. 3, pp. 299–310). Greenwich, CT: JAI.

Sackett, P. R., & Dreher, G. F. (1982). Constructs and assessment center dimensions: Some troubling empirical findings. *Journal of Applied Psychology, 67*, 401–410.

Sackett, P. R., & Tuzinski, K. A. (2001). The role of dimensions and exercises in assessment center judgments. In M. London (Ed.), *How people evaluate others in organizations* (pp. 111–129). Mahwah, NJ: Lawrence Erlbaum Associates, Inc.

Salas, E., Burke, S. C., Bowers, C. A., & Wilson, K. A. (2001). Team training in the skies: Does crew resource management (CRM) training work? *Human Factors, 43*, 641–674.

Salas, E., & Cannon-Bowers, J. A. (2001). The science of training: A decade of progress. *Annual Review of Psychology, 52*, 471–499.

Salas, E., Fowlkes, J. E., Stout, R. J., Milanovich, D. M., & Prince, C. (1999). Does CRM training improve teamwork skills in the cockpit? Two evaluation studies. *Human Factors, 41*, 326–343.

Sanchez, J. I., & Levine, E. L. (2001). The analysis of work in the 20th and 21st centuries. In N. Anderson, D. S. Ones, H. K. Sinangil, & C. Viswesvaran (Eds.), *International handbook of work and organizational psychology* (pp. 71–89). Thousand Oaks, CA: Sage.

Santos-Gomez, L. (1991). Knowledge acquisition and information searching strategies in diagnostic decision making. *Acta Psychologica, 77*, 293–305.

Singleton, T. M. (1978). Managerial motivation development: A study of college student leaders. *Academy of Management Journal, 21*, 493–498.

Slaski, M., & Cartwright, S. (2003). Emotional intelligence training and its implications for stress, health, and performance. *Stress and Health, 19*, 233–239.

Spychalski, A. C., Quiñones, M. A., Gaugler, B. B., & Pohley, K. (1997). A survey of assessment center practices in organizations in the United States. *Personnel Psychology, 50*, 71–90.

Tett, R. P., Guterman, H. A., Bleier, A., & Murphy, P. J. (2000). Development and content validation of a "hyperdimensional" taxonomy of managerial competence. *Human Performance, 13*, 205–251.

Thornton, G. C., III, & Byham, W. C. (1982). *Assessment centers and managerial performance.* New York: Academic Press.

Thornton, G. C., III, & Rogers, D. A. (2001, October). *Developmental assessment centers: Can we deliver the essential elements?* Paper presented at the 29th International Congress on Assessment Center Methods, Frankfurt, Germany.

Thornton, G. C., III, & Rupp, D. E. (2005). *Assessment centers in human resource management.* Mahwah, NJ: Lawrence Erlbaum Associates, Inc.

Tysoe, M. (1982). Social psychology and training techniques for industrial negotiators. *Industrial Relations Journal, 13*, 64–75.

Tziner, A., Ronen, S., & Hacohen, D. (1993). A four-year validation study of an assessment center in a financial corporation. *Journal of Organizational Behavior, 14*, 225–237.

Van Eerde, W. (2003). Procrastination at work and time management training. *Journal of Psychology: Interdisciplinary and Applied, 137*, 421–434.

Walter, M., & Thornton, G. C., III. (2004). *Measuring readiness to develop in a developmental assessment center.* Unpublished manuscript.

Waters, J. A. (1980). Managerial skill development. *Academy of Management Review, 5*, 449–453.

Wexley, K. N., & Baldwin, T. T. (1986). Management development. *Journal of Management, 12*, 277–294.

Wrenn, K. A., & Maurer, T. J. (2004). Beliefs about older workers' learning and development behavior in relation to beliefs about malleability of skills, age-related decline, and control. *Journal of Applied Social Psychology, 34*, 223–242.

Zuckerman, M., Gagne, M., & Nafshi, I. (2001). Pursuing academic interests: The role of implicit theories. *Journal of Applied Social Psychology, 31*, 2621–2631.

THE PSYCHOLOGIST-MANAGER JOURNAL, 2006, 9(2), 125–143

Perceptions of Managerial Performance Dimensions in Korea

Alyssa Mitchell Gibbons and Deborah E. Rupp
Department of Psychology
University of Illinois at Urbana-Champaign

Myungjoon Kim
Korean Psychological Testing Institute

Sang Eun Woo
Department of Psychology
University of Illinois at Urbana-Champaign

This article explores how cultural differences may affect the question of dimension choice for developmental assessment centers. A survey of over 300 Korean managers was used to investigate Korean perceptions of 20 dimensions commonly used in U.S. assessment centers. Factors included the importance of the dimensions, their perceived developability, Korean managers' interest in developing the dimensions, and the availability of opportunities to develop each dimension. Managers' free-response lists of important dimensions were also considered, exploring whether dimension models developed in the United States were likely to be adequate for Korean managers. Results indicate moderate but not perfect agreement with a previous study of U.S. managers (Gibbons, Rupp, Snyder, Holub, & Woo, this issue, p. 99). Korean managers indicated considerable interest in developing the dimensions but reported few opportunities to do so.

A developmental assessment center (DAC) is a collection of workplace simulation exercises and other assessments that are used to provide individuals with feedback and coaching on job-relevant behavioral dimensions (Thornton & Rupp, 2005; see also Carrick & Williams, 1999; Griffiths & Goodge, 1994; Jones & Whitmore, 1995; G. Lee, 2000, 2003; Povah, 1986). DACs have been used for some time in

---

Correspondence should be sent to Deborah E. Rupp, Department of Psychology and Institute of Labor and Industrial Relations, University of Illinois at Urbana-Champaign, 603 East Daniel Street, Champaign, IL 61820. E-mail: derupp@uiuc.edu

the United Kingdom (G. Lee, 2000) and are increasingly prevalent in U.S. organizations (Kudisch et al., 2001). Recent evidence showing increased interest in the assessment center method (M. J. Kim, 2004; S. K. Kim, 1998; Min, 2004) and managerial development (Cho, 1998; S. Park, 2003) suggests that DACs may offer an effective tool for competitive Eastern nations such as Korea.

Thus far, the popularity of DACs appears to rest on the reputation of traditional assessment centers (ACs; Carrick & Williams, 1999), which have been repeatedly shown to be effective for selection or promotion (e.g., Gaugler, Rosenthal, Thornton, & Bentson, 1987; Howard, 1997; Spychalski, Quiñones, Gaugler, & Pohley, 1997; Thornton & Rupp, 2005). Yet ACs and DACs differ in many fundamental ways, including the role of the assessors and the nature of the feedback provided to participants (Thornton & Rogers, 2001). As a result, it may be inappropriate to assume that results from one will necessarily generalize to the other (Carrick & Williams, 1999) or that a program designed as an AC can be used for development without modification (Thornton & Rupp, 2005). Further, cultural differences have frequently been shown to affect development (e.g., Earley, 1994; Hofstede, 1986; Jaeger, 1986; Morris & Pavett, 1992; Newman & Nollen, 1996). Before DACs can be used effectively by Korean organizations, empirical research is needed to determine whether and how they may need to be modified to be appropriate for that culture.

The Korean business climate is rapidly changing. In the wake of the 1997 Asian economic crisis, organizations and individuals have become more competitive, with a greater emphasis on management development than ever before. Consequently, a number of major Korean organizations, including Samsung and LG, have implemented competency-based human resource management programs to help their managers develop necessary skills (Bak & Uhm, 1998). Such programs represent a significant departure from traditional Korean views of management, in which managerial ability is believed to be innate and job security can be taken for granted (Cho, 1998; S. Park, 2003). It also reflects a major trend away from group-based and seniority-based human resource management and toward more individualized and job-focused approaches, such as competency modeling (H. J. Kim, 2001; H. J. Kim, 2003). However, such changes in Korean organizations are in just the beginning stages and are still a novel experience for most Korean managers. This tension between traditional views and contemporary needs for competitiveness and improvement presents a potential challenge in the design of DACs (and other development programs) in Korea.

Further, although Korean organizations are increasingly adopting management approaches from Western nations, Korean culture in general is different in many ways from the U.S. and British cultures in which DACs developed. For example, Korean social norms emphasize social harmony, sympathy, and hierarchy (Choi & Han, 1998; Choi & Park, 1990; Han, 2000; J. E. Kim, 1987), but U.S. culture is generally considered to be individualist and egalitarian (e.g., Hofstede, 1980,

1991). Korean managers tend to be relationship oriented but authoritarian at the same time (Choi & Park, 1990). These differences may affect not only the respective definitions of effective management in each culture but also the way in which managers respond to and participate in development efforts (cf. Earley, 1994; Newman & Nollen, 1996).

The purpose of the current study is to explore what behavioral dimensions might best be assessed and developed within managerial DACs conducted in Korea. The choice of dimensions to be assessed is one of the first steps in designing any AC or DAC (International Task Force on Assessment Center Guidelines, 2000; Thornton & Mueller-Hanson, 2004; Thornton & Rupp, 2005); it is consequently a logical first place to begin filling the research gap regarding DACs. Although research regarding DACs is increasing (Howard, 1997), we are aware of only one other study that considered the question of dimension choice (Gibbons, Rupp, Snyder, Holub, & Woo, this issue, p. 99) and none that considered it cross-culturally.

DAC DIMENSIONS

Dimensions are "meaningful and relevant categories" (International Task Force on Assessment Center Guidelines, 2000, p. 320) into which the behaviors observed in an AC can be classified, chosen to reflect the competency requirements of the job in question. For example, the dimensions in a managerial AC might include leadership or communication skills. Dimensions are clusters of behaviors in which the individual behavioral elements are quite specific but the overall category represents types of behavior that are likely to occur across situations. This approach allows much richer feedback than that from a global rating or pass–fail evaluation, which gives the participant little information about how to improve (Arnold, 1987; Griffiths & Allen, 1987).

Although commonly accepted guidelines (International Task Force on Assessment Center Guidelines, 2000) recommend that dimensions be chosen for a specific position based on job analysis, researchers have identified a number of dimensions that appear to be common to most managerial ACs (Gaugler, Bentson, & Pohley, 1990). Unfortunately for DACs, the majority of this research focuses on the efficacy of these dimensions for prediction (e.g., Howard & Bray, 1988) rather than whether the dimensions may be developable (Jones & Whitmore, 1995). For development to occur, DACs require dimensions on which performance can reasonably be expected to change given time and effort (Rupp, Snyder, Gibbons, & Thornton, this issue, p.75; Thornton & Rogers, 2001). Further, it matters not only whether the dimensions are objectively developable but also whether they are perceived as being developable. Research indicates that individuals' lay theories about the changeability of various attributes influence their development behavior in relation to those attributes (e.g., Dunning, 1995; Dweck & Leggett, 1988; Zuckerman, Gagne, & Nafshi, 2001).

The current study sought to identify developable dimensions of general managerial performance in Korea, in light of the nation's growing interest in managerial development (e.g., S. K. Kim, 1998). We began with common AC dimensions identified in a study of U.S. managers (Gibbons et al., this issue, p. 99); confirmed their relevance for Korean managers, with a review of the Korean literature; and included other variables of interest to potential DAC developers, such as Korean managers' interest in developing the dimensions and their availability of opportunities to develop each dimension. Our purpose is not to present a definitive model of performance for all Korean managerial DACs but rather to provide information regarding common dimensions that are likely to emerge in many job analyses.

RESEARCH ON DAC DIMENSIONS IN THE U.S.

Gibbons et al. (this issue, p. 99) identified likely DAC dimensions based on a comprehensive literature review, subject matter expert ratings, and a survey of U.S. managers. They found 16 behavioral dimensions that were considered important and developable (see Table 1). Gibbons et al. also suggested four nontraditional dimensions from the research literature that may be amenable to development via

TABLE 1
Common Managerial Performance Dimensions

Traditional U.S. Dimensions	Nontraditional Dimensions
Problem solving	Readiness to develop[a]
Information seeking[a]	Fairness
Creativity[a]	Emotion management[a]
Planning and organizing[a]	Cultural adaptability[a]
Adaptability	
Stress tolerance	
Conscientiousness	
Motivation[a]	
Oral communication[a]	
Written communication[a]	
Listening	
Persuasiveness	
Relationship/interpersonal skills[a]	
Leadership[a]	
Teamwork[a]	
Conflict management/resolution	

Note. From Gibbons, Rupp, Snyder, Holub, and Woo (this issue, p. 99).
[a]Dimensions supported by prior research on Korean culture and management (J. M. Kim, 2001a, 2001b; Ko, 2002; D. M. Lee, 2002; S. Lee et al., 2002; J. Park, 2001; N. Park, 1995; Song, 2001).

DACs: fairness, emotion management, readiness to develop, and cultural adapt-ability. They found that American managers also considered these dimensions to be important and developable. This study provided useful information for those designing and developing DACs, but it focused exclusively on U.S. managers. If DACs are to be used in other cultures, it is necessary to determine what dimensions are seen as important and developable within those cultures.

RESEARCH ON DIMENSIONS IN KOREA

To reconcile the dimensions suggested in the research conducted in the United States with the Korean management literature, we conducted a literature search of Korean journals using the Korean National Database. The Korean management lit-erature suggests that many of the developable performance dimensions proposed by Gibbons et al. (this issue, p. 99) are relevant to managerial effectiveness in Ko-rea. Dimensions from the U.S. list that were important in the Korean literature in-cluded information seeking, communication, problem solving, leadership, motiva-tion, creativity, and teamwork (J. M. Kim, 2001a, 2001b; Ko, 2002; D. M. Lee, 2002; S. Lee et al., 2002; J. Park, 2001; N. Park, 1995). Information seeking, prob-lem solving, planning and organizing, interpersonal relationships, and teamwork were further identified as training and development needs of Korean managers (Song, 2001). Two of the nontraditional dimensions suggested by Gibbons et al. were supported in the Korean literature. S. Lee et al. (2002) listed emotional stabil-ity as a critical skill, similar to Gibbons et al.'s emotion management. Given the current emphasis on management development within Korean organizations (Bak & Uhm, 1998; Cho, 1998), readiness to develop appears to be an important dimen-sion for Korean managers.

RESEARCH AIMS

This study sought to identify developable behavioral dimensions relevant to Ko-rean managers to provide a stepping-stone on which research on international DACs can be built. We use the term *stepping-stone* because the best way to deter-mine if dimensions are important and developable is to use them in a DAC and con-duct a validity study. However, to conduct such a study, DACs must be developed, and to develop a DAC, there must be a determination of what dimensions are rele-vant and developable. Unfortunately, few DAC validity studies exist offering evi-dence on the effectiveness of DACs for fostering dimension-level improvement. Hence, the current study goes one step further in this research stream.

The goals of our study were to identify the dimensions most important to Ko-rean managers, determine the degree to which Korean managers believe the di-mensions to be developable, compare the responses of Korean managers to those of U.S. managers (from Gibbons et al., this issue, p. 99), and assess the interest of Korean managers in developing these dimensions and their opportunities to do so.

METHODS

Participants

Surveys were administered to managers in 11 South Korean organizations. Of the 545 managers solicited, 317 returned completed surveys, for a response rate of 58%. Most (47%) were responsible for 10 or fewer employees, though 5% managed 100 people or more. Manufacturing, finance, service, transportation, retail, and construction sectors were represented.

Survey

The survey included an open-ended measure asking respondents to list 10 skills critical for managerial success; a list of the dimensions and their definitions; and scales measuring managerial importance, general importance, developability, opportunity to develop, and interest in developing (see Table 2). Each scale contained 4–10 items, which participants answered for each of the 20 dimensions. All items used 7-point Likert-type response scales from 1 (*strongly disagree*) to 7 (*strongly agree*). The managerial importance scale measured the degree to which participants considered the dimension necessary for effective performance in a manage-

TABLE 2
Scale Reliabilities

Scale	Sample Item	No. of Items	Average Alpha	Minimum Alpha	Maximum Alpha
Managerial importance	*I use this skill on a daily basis.*	6	.87	.81	.89
General importance	*This skill is important for success in any job.*	4	.85	.78	.89
Developability	*Managers should improve this skill throughout their careers.*	5	.73	.68	.78
Opportunity to develop	*I have received formal training (classes, seminars, etc.) in this skill since I was hired.*	5	.91	.89	.92
Interest in developing	*Improving this skill further would be very useful to me in my career right now.*	6	.88	.84	.90

rial position, whereas the general importance scale measured importance for jobs in general. The developability scale items explored the degree to which participants expected performance on the dimension to improve with time and effort. The opportunity scale asked about the availability of formal and informal opportunities to develop the dimension, and the interest scale assessed respondents' attitudes toward improving themselves on the dimension. Items regarding training experiences, motivation for training,[1] and demographic and background information were included. The survey was originally written in English. It was translated, backtranslated, modified, and evaluated according to current guidelines governing this practice (Coyne, 2000).

RESULTS

Reliability

Reliability estimates for the five scales were determined by calculating Cronbach's alpha coefficient independently for each of the 20 dimensions. Six items were dropped due to irresolvable negative correlations with other items in the same scale. Items were dropped only if the negative correlations occurred on multiple dimensions, and dropped items were removed from scales for all dimensions to preserve consistency. Alpha coefficients for each finalized scale were averaged across all dimensions to obtain an overall reliability estimate (see Table 2). All five scales have acceptable levels of reliability (Nunnally & Bernstein, 1994), which appear to be reasonably consistent across the 20 dimensions.

Perceived Importance of Dimensions

Participants' average managerial importance ratings of all dimensions were above the scale midpoint (4 on a 7-point scale). A series of one-sample t tests comparing the observed mean for each dimension to the neutral value (4) indicated that the means for all dimensions were significantly greater than the neutral value, even after using the Bonferroni correction for multiple comparisons (corrected $\alpha = .002$, corresponding to an original α of .05). The same result was observed for the general importance scale, with mean ratings for all dimensions significantly exceeding 4. All dimensions are listed in rank order of rated managerial importance in Table 3. Leadership, conscientiousness, problem solving, and teamwork were the dimensions rated most important by survey respondents. Of the nontraditional dimensions, readiness to develop and fairness were rated as being more important than many traditional dimensions, though emotion management and cultural

---

[1]Due to space limitations, these items are not discussed in the present article.

TABLE 3

Korean Managers' Ratings of Managerial Importance (MI), General Importance (GI), Developability (D), Opportunity (O), and Interest (I)

Dimension	MI Rating	MI Score Ranking	GI Rating	GI Score Ranking	D Rating	D Score Ranking	O Rating	O Score Ranking	I Rating	I Score Ranking
Leadership	5.80	1	5.66	2	5.28	1	4.19	1	5.67	1
Conscientiousness	5.71	2	5.85	1	4.53	17	3.48[b]	16	5.19	10
Problem solving	5.69	3	5.64	3	5.23	2	4.03	3	5.52	2
Teamwork	5.56	4	5.50	4	5.06	4	4.10	2	5.31	8
Relationship/interpersonal skills	5.53	5	5.44	5	4.82	11	3.78[b]	8	5.36	6
Planning and organizing	5.41	6	5.22	11	5.19	3	3.89	6	5.31	9
Motivation	5.35	7	5.34	10	4.89	6	3.88	7	5.07	15
Readiness to develop[a]	5.35	8	5.44	6	4.84	9	3.99	4	5.44	3
Conflict management/resolution	5.33	9	5.41	7	4.92	5	3.70[b]	9	5.41	5
Information seeking	5.33	10	5.17	13	4.88	7	3.63[b]	11	5.33	7
Fairness[a]	5.28	11	5.40	8	4.61	16	3.45[b]	17	5.17	12
Persuasiveness	5.27	12	5.12	15	4.82	12	3.58[b]	13	5.19	11
Listening	5.23	13	5.21	12	4.75	13	3.62[b]	12	5.09	13
Creativity	5.23	14	5.40	9	4.65	15	3.56[b]	15	5.43	4
General adaptability	5.18	15	5.17	14	4.84	10	3.66[b]	10	4.98	17
Oral communication	5.17	16	4.98	16	4.75	14	3.58[b]	14	5.08	14
Emotion management[a]	4.97	17	4.94	17	4.41	18	3.20[b]	20	4.99	16
Stress management	4.83	18	4.88	18	4.40	19	3.33[b]	19	4.90	18
Written communication	4.83	19	4.63	20	4.87	8	3.92	5	4.75	20
Cultural adaptability[a]	4.69	20	4.70	19	4.40	20	3.45[b]	18	4.76	19

Note.   Ratings are mean scores on a scale consisting of 7-point Likert-type items, with higher scores indicating higher levels of agreement. Rankings are derived from the mean ratings.

[a]Nontraditional dimension.

[b]Opportunity mean is significantly less than 4.0, $p < .001$.

adaptability were among the dimensions rated as least important. Nevertheless, Korean managers did perceive these dimensions as being at least somewhat relevant.

None of the dimensions was found to be significantly different from the dimensions immediately preceding or succeeding it in rank. However, dimensions at the upper end of the rankings were significantly different from those at the lower end. The dimensions can be grouped into slightly overlapping clusters, as represented in Figure 1. Dimensions within the same circle are not significantly different from each other; all other differences are statistically significant ($p \leq .002$). Dimensions are shown in descending order by managerial importance score.

Perceived Developability of Dimensions

Participants' ratings of developability were also significantly above the neutral point for all dimensions (all $p < .001$; see Table 3). The dimensions perceived as being most amenable to development were leadership, problem solving, and planning and organizing. Again, no dimension was significantly different in perceived developability from the dimensions closest to it, but significant differences were observed between dimensions farther apart on the developability continuum. Figure 2 shows the differences between dimensions, with dimensions in the same circle not significantly different from each other (i.e., $p > .002$ for dimensions in the same circle). Several of the dimensions identified as being most important were rated as being highly developable, but others showed sizable discrepancies. Conscientiousness, which received the second-highest managerial importance rating, was perceived as one of the least developable dimensions.

Open-Ended Responses

Participants' responses to the open-ended section of the survey, in which they were asked to list 10 skills critical for managerial success (not necessarily in order), were translated into English, and responses with essentially the same meaning (e.g., "leading people," "leadership") were grouped together. There was considerable agreement among the Korean managers: a total of 99 distinct terms emerged out of over 2,800 responses. Three raters then coded these 99 response categories to determine whether they matched the survey dimensions. All three raters agreed on 61% of the categories, and at least two raters agreed on 94%. Any remaining disagreements were resolved by discussion. Table 4 illustrates the frequency of open-ended responses that matched the survey dimensions. Consistent with other results, leadership was the most commonly identified dimension, occurring 321 times in total (some respondents identified multiple components of the definition of leadership, such as providing vision or supporting subordinates). Of the 2,867

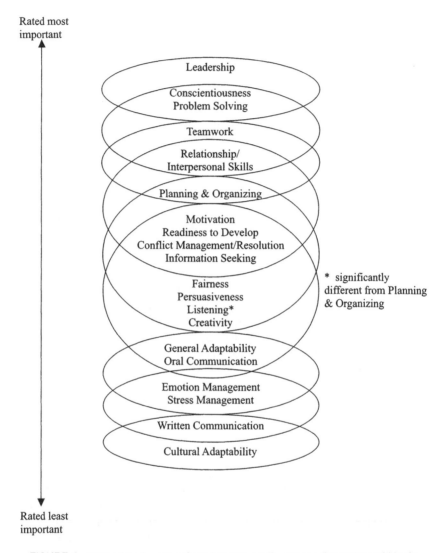

Rated most
important

Leadership

Conscientiousness
Problem Solving

Teamwork

Relationship/
Interpersonal Skills

Planning & Organizing

Motivation
Readiness to Develop
Conflict Management/Resolution
Information Seeking

Fairness
Persuasiveness
Listening*
Creativity

* significantly
different from Planning
& Organizing

General Adaptability
Oral Communication

Emotion Management
Stress Management

Written Communication

Cultural Adaptability

Rated least
important

FIGURE 1 Dimensions in order of rated managerial importance. Dimensions within the same circle are not significantly different from each other (critical α =.002, using the Bonferroni correction for multiple comparisons).

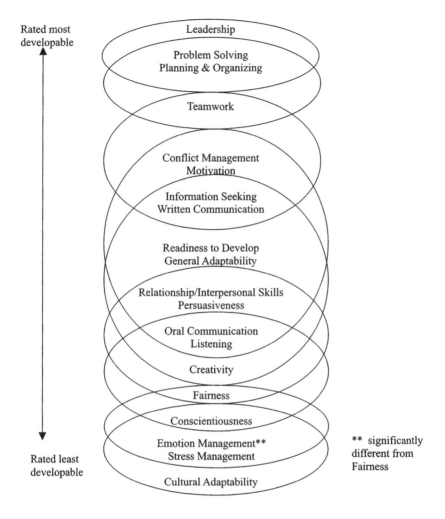

Rated most
developable

Leadership

Problem Solving
Planning & Organizing

Teamwork

Conflict Management
Motivation

Information Seeking
Written Communication

Readiness to Develop
General Adaptability

Relationship/Interpersonal Skills
Persuasiveness

Oral Communication
Listening

Creativity

Fairness

Conscientiousness

Emotion Management**
Stress Management

** significantly
different from
Fairness

Rated least
developable

Cultural Adaptability

FIGURE 2 Dimensions in order of rated developability. Dimensions within the same circle
are not significantly different from each other (critical α =.002, using the Bonferroni correction
for multiple comparisons).

TABLE 4
Comparison of Importance and Developability by Ratings and Free Responses to U.S. Managers' Ratings

Dimension	MI Rating	Free-Response Frequency	U.S. Rating Order[a]	D Rating Order	U.S. D Rating Order[a]
Leadership	5.80	321	1	1	9
Conscientiousness	5.71	210	10	17	15
Problem solving	5.69	218	3	2	7
Teamwork	5.56	145	4	4	3
Relationship/interpersonal skills	5.53	147	14	11	11
Planning and organizing	5.41	139	2	3	2
Motivation	5.35	105	15	6	19
Readiness to develop	5.35	121	16	9	16
Conflict management/resolution	5.33	5	5	5	6
Information seeking	5.33	119	13	7	4
Fairness	5.28	203	8	16	12
Persuasiveness	5.27	66	18	12	17
Creativity	5.23	172	19	13	20
Listening	5.23	100	9	15	8
General adaptability	5.18	71	7	10	14
Oral communication	5.17	55	6	14	5
Emotion management	4.97	45	20	18	18
Stress management	4.97	29	11	19	10
Written communication	4.83	47	17	8	1
Cultural adaptability	4.69	0	12	20	13

Note. MI = managerial importance; D = developability.
[a]From Gibbons, Rupp, Snyder, Holub, and Woo (this issue, p. 99).

open-ended responses received, 2,318 (81%) were classified into 1 of the 20 survey dimensions.

Three of the authors evaluated the remaining responses in an effort to identify dimensions or general themes relevant to management in Korea that might have been overlooked due to the U.S. origin of the original set of dimensions. One of the most prevalent themes related to general business knowledge. This dimension could easily have appeared among the U.S. dimensions; it was excluded from the original list used by Gibbons et al. (this issue, p. 99) because it was considered to be beyond the scope of a DAC. Responses such as "conducting business" and "knowledge of general management" occurred 203 times. Seventy-one responses listed "understanding of an organization" as an important dimension, but this response appears to refer to understanding of one's particular organization: It generally occurred with the other business-knowledge items, suggesting that participants considered it to be distinct. Another strong theme was that of company loyalty. Many respondents (164) explicitly described "loyalty to an organization" or "attaching oneself to an organization" as a critical skill for managers. Other, less prevalent themes included trust building, or reassuring others that one has their best interests at heart, which was mentioned by 33 respondents, and self-discipline, or maintaining a healthy self-controlled approach to life and work, which appeared in 21 responses.

Comparison of Korean and U.S. Managers

Table 4 compares the Korean managers' perceptions about the dimensions to those of the U.S. managers surveyed by Gibbons et al. (this issue, p. 99). Because the two studies used different rating scales and different items to measure importance and developability, Table 4 presents the rank order of the dimensions based on the appropriate ratings (readers interested in the precise means are referred to Gibbons et al. and to Table 3). The Pearson correlation coefficient between the U.S. importance ratings and the Korean managerial importance ratings was $r = .40, p > .05$. Though this correlation is not statistically significant, it is important to note that the analysis was performed on the overall average ratings for the two samples, so the "sample size" involved is only the number of dimensions ($N = 20$). This suggests that there exists a moderate, but not perfect, degree of agreement between Korean and U.S. managers. Both groups agreed that leadership, problem solving, and teamwork were among the most important dimensions. The greatest discrepancies involved oral communication, which was rated the 6th most important dimension by U.S. managers but rated 16th by Korean managers, and relationship/interpersonal skills, which was rated 5th by Korean managers but only 14th by U.S. managers. The Pearson correlation between Korean and U.S. ratings of developability was stronger but still moderate, $r = .49, p < .05$. Large discrepancies involved oral communication, stress management, and cultural adaptability, which

TABLE 5
Correlations Between Scales

	MI	GI	D	O	I
Managerial importance (MI)	1.00				
General importance (GI)	0.71	1.00			
Developability (D)	0.59	0.52	1.00		
Opportunity to develop (O)	0.23	0.16	0.43	1.00	
Interest in developing (I)	0.61	0.63	0.56	0.23	1.00

were rated the 5th, 10th, and 13th most developable dimensions, respectively, by U.S. managers but rated 13th, 19th, and 20th in developability by Korean respondents. Conversely, motivation was considered fairly developable (rated 6th) by Korean managers but not by U.S. managers (rated 19th).

Opportunity and Interest

Ratings of interest in development were all significantly greater than 4 (see Table 3). Korean managers were most interested in developing leadership, problem solving, readiness to develop, creativity, and conflict management/resolution. However, opportunity scale ratings were not significantly above the neutral point. In fact, 13 of the 20 dimensions had opportunity scores significantly below 4 ($p < .001$), indicating that Korean managers perceived few available avenues to develop these dimensions. The other seven dimensions were statistically equal to 4. Creativity and conflict management, though among the five dimensions that Korean managers expressed most interest in developing, were both among the dimensions for which opportunity to develop was rated negatively. Correlations among the average ratings for each dimension on each of the five scales are reported in Table 5.

DISCUSSION

The present study suggests that Korean managers' beliefs about managerial performance are in many ways similar, but not identical, to those of their U.S. counterparts. Korean managers believed that all 20 dimensions listed in the survey were at least somewhat important for managerial success. This list included all of the traditional and nontraditional U.S. dimensions suggested by Gibbons et al. (this issue, p. 99), even those that were not explicitly identified in the Korean literature. The most important dimensions for Korean managers were leadership, conscientiousness, problem solving, and planning and organizing, which emerged consistently across multiple methods of assessment (ratings and free responses). Overall, the 20 survey dimensions accounted for the bulk of the dimensions spontaneously identified by Korean managers. The primary exception was the dimension of business knowledge, which is certainly applicable to U.S. managers as well as Korean managers, though it might be difficult to develop effectively within the limited time frame of a DAC. Further, Korean managers indicated that all 20 dimensions could be developed with time and effort, though some were seen as being more developable than others. Leadership, problem solving, and planning and organizing were considered highly developable. Dimensions considered highly important, developable, and interesting should be expected to offer the greatest return in terms of relevance, improvement, and participation. Leadership and problem solving, which appeared among the top five dimensions on all of these measures, appeared to be the most critical dimensions for a Korean DAC.

Korean managers expressed interest in developing all dimensions, especially the dimensions that they perceived as being important, but rated the availability of development opportunities as neutral at best. Opportunity to develop was highly correlated with perceived developability but only moderately with importance, suggesting that development opportunities may be targeted more to the dimensions on which improvement is most expected rather than those on which it is most needed. Although it would be impractical to design development interventions for skills that could not be developed at all, participants believed that all dimensions were at least somewhat developable. It should therefore be possible to create development opportunities for the most important dimensions as well as the easiest to develop.

Study Strengths

This study provides evidence that the dimensions commonly used in U.S. assessment centers are also perceived as being important in Korea. Further, it shows that these dimensions are believed to be developable given time and effort, which is a necessary condition of inclusion in DACs. It also provides information regarding the current state of managerial development opportunities in Korea and managers' interest in these opportunities.

A particular strength of the present study is the breadth of its sample. Managers who completed the survey varied considerably in age, experience, and management level and represented 11 organizations in a variety of industries. This variance provides reason to believe that the results are reasonably representative of Korean managers in general. The study also used multiple methods to assess perceptions of importance (rating and free response) and reliable multi-item measures to assess other constructs.

Limitations

One limitation of the study is its exclusive focus on Korea. Although some comparisons can be made to existing work on U.S. managers, it was not possible to compare the two groups directly. Further, Korea and the United States are not representative of all cultures. Another limitation is that the results reflect only managers' beliefs about the dimensions. The degree to which these dimensions can be developed via DACs has yet to be empirically tested. However, our results provide a starting point for future DAC research by suggesting dimensions that are likely to prove developable.

Future Research

Future research should continue to assess the appropriateness of DAC dimensions in various cultures, making efforts to identify dimensions specific to the cultures studied and subjecting all dimensions to cross-cultural validation. This process may reveal dimensions that are general across most cultures as well as dimensions specific to a particular culture or group of cultures.

This study is a first step toward determining the validity of DACs for producing actual improvement in managerial performance. To achieve this goal, DACs must be designed and built in a variety of contexts and cultures. The findings of the present study suggest that DACs in the United States and Korea may use similar dimensions, but it remains important to consider cultural factors in other aspects of DAC design, such as standards for effective performance and feedback. DAC effectiveness must be measured longitudinally. Improvement in the DAC is valuable only if it can be shown to transfer to the workplace and persist over time.

The present article provides information about potential dimensions for Korean DACs and illustrates a strategy for identifying appropriate dimensions in other cultures. Dimensions used in traditional ACs in the United States were perceived as being important and developable by Korean managers, suggesting that these dimensions may be appropriate for Korean DACs as well, though cultural differences did appear in the amount of emphasis placed on various dimensions. Further attention to cultural issues is needed as DAC designers choose dimensions and go on to validate their programs.

ACKNOWLEDGMENTS

Alyssa Gibbons is supported under a National Science Foundation Graduate Research Fellowship. Any opinions, findings, conclusions, or recommendations expressed in this publication are those of the authors and do not necessarily reflect the views of the National Science Foundation.

The first and second author contributed equally to this study. Portions of this article were presented at the 20th annual meeting of the Society for Industrial and Organizational Psychology, Los Angeles, 2005.

We thank the staff of the Korean Psychological Testing Institute for their assistance with this project.

REFERENCES

Arnold, G. T. (1987). Feedback and career development. In H. W. More & R. C. Unsinger (Eds.), *The police assessment center* (pp. 167–201). Springfield, IL: Charles C. Thomas.

Bak, P., & Uhm, D. (1998). *Human resources development of white-collar workers in the era of infinite competition.* Retrieved December 24, 2003, from the Samsung Economic Research Institute Web site: http://www.seri.org/db/dbRptV.html?s_menu=0101&pub _key=db19980905

Carrick, P., & Williams, R. (1999). Development centres—A review of assumptions. *Human Resource Management Journal, 9*(2), 77–92.

Cho, B. (1998). Education of starting business and effective instructional methods. *Management Education Research, 2*(2), 27–48.

Choi, S., & Han, G. (1998). Social psychology of Korean people reflected in their interpersonal behaviors. In International Society for Korean Studies (Ed.), *Koreans and Korean Culture* (pp. 161–193). Seoul, Korea: Sagyejul.

Choi, S., & Park, S. (1990, November). Social psychological analysis of "we-ness." Paper presented at the annual meeting of the Korean Psychological Association.

Coyne, I. (2000). International Test Commission test adaptation guidelines. Retrieved April 21, 2000, from the International Test Commission Web site: http://www.intestcom.org/test_adaptation.htm

Dunning, D. (1995). Trait importance and modifiability as factors influencing self-assessment and self-enhancement motives. *Personality and Social Psychology Bulletin, 21*, 1297–1306.

Dweck, C. S., & Leggett, E. L. (1988). A social-cognitive approach to motivation and personality. *Psychological Review, 95*, 256–273.

Earley, P. C. (1994). Self or group? Cultural effects of training on self-efficacy and performance. *Administrative Science Quarterly, 39*, 89–117.

Gaugler, B. B., Bentson, C., & Pohley, K. (1990). *A survey of assessment center practices in organizations.* Unpublished manuscript.

Gaugler, B. B., Rosenthal, D. B., Thornton, G. C., III, & Bentson, C. (1987). Meta-analysis of assessment center validity. *Journal of Applied Psychology, 72*, 493–511.

Griffiths, P., & Allen, B. (1987). Assessment centres: Breaking with tradition. *Journal of Management Development, 6*(1), 18–29.

Griffiths, P., & Goodge, P. (1994). Development centres: The third generation. *Personnel Management, 26*, 40–43.

Han, G. (2000). Social spheres (public and private) of Korean society: Conflict of justice discourse and relationship discourse. *Korean Journal of Psychological and Social Issues, 6*(2), 39–63.

Hofstede, G. (1980). *Culture's consequence: International differences in work-related values.* Newbury Park, CA: Sage.

Hofstede, G. (1986). Cultural differences in teaching and learning. *International Journal of Intercultural Relations, 10*, 301–320.

Hofstede, G. (1991). *Cultures and organizations: Software of the mind.* New York: McGraw-Hill.

Howard, A. (1997). A reassessment of assessment centers: Challenges for the 21st century. *Journal of Social Behavior and Personality, 12*, 13–52.

Howard, A., & Bray, D. W. (1988). *Managerial lives in transition: Advancing age and changing times.* New York: Guilford.

International Task Force on Assessment Center Guidelines. (2000). Guidelines and ethical considerations for assessment center operations. *Public Personnel Management, 29*, 315–331.

Jaeger, A. M. (1986). Organization development and national culture: Where's the fit? *Academy of Management Review, 11*, 178–190.

Jones, R. G., & Whitmore, M. D. (1995). Evaluating developmental assessment centers as interventions. *Personnel Psychology, 48*, 377–388.

Kim, H. J. (2001). *Changes in organizational culture of large enterprises in Korea.* Unpublished doctoral dissertation, Korea University, Seoul.

Kim, H. J. (2003). Introduction and development of competency-based human resource management (CBHRM) for Korean firms. *Posco Research Institute: POSRI Management Research, 3*(1), 120–158.

Kim, J. E. (1987). *Mentality and behavioral patterns of Korean.* Seoul, Korea: Ewha Womans University.

Kim, J. M. (2001a). Developing a curriculum centered on competency for developing the human resources of an enterprise. *Journal of Vocational Education Research, 20*(2), 109–128.

Kim, J. M. (2001b). Identification of job competencies in developing human resource: The case of a company which provides a preschool education program. *Korean Journal of Agricultural Extension, 8*, 159–177.

Kim, M. J. (2004, November). *Developmental assessment centers.* Paper presented at the congress of the Society for Korean Industrial and Organizational Psychology, Seoul, Korea.

Kim, S. K. (1998). Assessment center method—Its nature and applications. *Ewha Management Review, 16*, 61–78.

Ko, J. (2002). *The competency modeling for improved task performance and an analysis on training needs for the competency development—In the case of manufacturer.* Unpublished master's thesis, Korea University, Seoul.

Kudisch, J. D., Avis, J. M., Fallon, J. D., Thibodeaux, H. F., Roberts, F. E., Rollier, T. J., et al. (2001, April). *A survey of assessment center practices in organizations worldwide: Maximizing innovation or business as usual?* Paper presented at the 16th annual conference of the Society for Industrial Organizational Psychology, San Diego, CA.

Lee, D. M. (2002). Information technology and the changing role of middle management. *Management Research, 9*(1), 21–36.

Lee, G. (2000). The state of the art in development centres. *Selection and Development Review, 16*(1), 10–14.

Lee, G. (2003). Same old development centres? *Selection and Development Review, 19*(5), 3–6.

Lee, S., Kim, M., Kim, C., Park, J., Sul, H., Yoo, T., et al. (2002). Development of evaluation factors for selecting government managers. *Korean Journal of Industrial and Organizational Psychology, 15*(3), 23–47.

Min, B. M. (2004, November). *Assessment center methods in Korea: Cases and issues.* Presented at the congress of the Society for Korean Industrial and Organizational Psychology, Seoul, Korea.

Morris, T., & Pavett, C. M. (1992). Management style and productivity in two cultures. *Journal of International Business Studies, 23*, 169–179.

Newman, K. L., & Nollen, S. D. (1996). Culture and congruence: The fit between management practices and national culture. *Journal of International Business Studies, 27*, 753–779.

Nunnally, J. C., & Bernstein, I. H. (1994). *Psychometric theory* (3rd ed.). New York: McGraw-Hill.

Park, J. (2001). A cross-cultural psychology study on the globalization—Focusing on the core competencies according to organizational cultures. *Yongnam University: Yongnam Regional Development Research, 27*, 33–49.

Park, N. (1995). Strategies for improving leadership competency through manager development. *Sogang Management Research, 6*(1), 101.

Park, S. (2003). *Can managerial skills be learned and taught? A study on the multimedia business simulation.* Unpublished doctoral dissertation, Yonsei University, Seoul, Korea.

Povah, N. (1986). Using assessment centres as a means for self-development. *Industrial and Commercial Training, 18*(2), 22–25.

Song, J. (2001). *Training and development needs to develop business core competencies.* Unpublished master's thesis, Korea University, Seoul, Korea.

Spychalski, A. C., Quiñones, M. A., Gaugler, B. B., & Pohley, K. (1997). A survey of assessment center practices in organizations in the United States. *Personnel Psychology, 50*, 71–90.

Thornton, G. C., III, & Mueller-Hanson, R. A. (2004). *Developing organizational simulations: A guide for practitioners and students.* Mahwah, NJ: Lawrence Erlbaum Associates, Inc.

Thornton, G. C., III, & Rogers, D. A. (2001, October). *Developmental assessment centers: Can we deliver the essential elements?* Paper presented at the 29th International Congress on Assessment Center Methods, Frankfurt, Germany.

Thornton, G. C., III, & Rupp, D. E. (2005). *Assessment centers in human resource management.* Mahwah, NJ: Lawrence Erlbaum Associates, Inc.

Zuckerman, M., Gagne, M., & Nafshi, I. (2001). Pursuing academic interests: The role of implicit theories. *Journal of Applied Social Psychology, 31,* 2621–2631.

THE PSYCHOLOGIST-MANAGER JOURNAL, 2006, 9(2), 145–170

Using Developmental Assessment Centers to Foster Workplace Fairness

Deborah E. Rupp, Amanda Baldwin, and Michael Bashshur

Department of Psychology
University of Illinois at Urbana-Champaign

Developmental assessment centers (DACs) have become a popular means for providing coaching, feedback, and experiential learning opportunities for managers. Typically, these programs focus on traditional leadership competencies such as communication, problem solving, and conflict management. The purpose of this article is to encourage psychologist-managers to consider the DAC method for fostering development in the area of fairness. After reviewing the DAC method, we discuss the concept of organizational justice (fairness) and its impact on employee attitudes and performance. We then provide an illustration of how a DAC program to develop fairness skills might be designed and implemented.

Selecting a training method for any purpose requires the consideration of many factors, including the length of time available for the training, constraints in the physical environment in which the training will take place, and the characteristics of both the trainees and the organization. Given ample time and available resources, all training programs should have several characteristics. That is, a training program should in some way present the information or concepts to be learned, demonstrate the skills or dimensions to be learned, allow trainees the opportunity to practice what they learned, and provide feedback during and after practice (Salas & Cannon-Bowers, 2001). There are many commonly applied approaches to training, such as information presentation, modeling, simulation, lectures, conferences, computer-assisted instruction, case studies, role-playing, group exercises, orientations, apprenticeships, and mentoring (Campbell & Kuncel, 2001). An excellent approach that combines several of these formats is the developmental assessment center method.

Correspondence should be sent to Deborah E. Rupp, Department of Psychology and Institute of Labor and Industrial Relations, University of Illinois at Urbana-Champaign, 603 East Daniel Street, Champaign, IL 61820. E-mail: derupp@uiuc.edu

Assessment centers (ACs) are a widely used method of assessment in which people participate in multiple simulation exercises (e.g, leaderless group discussions, in-basket exercises, role-plays). A panel of trained assessors measures performance on a given set of behavioral dimensions, and performance feedback is provided (Griffiths & Allen, 1987; Thornton & Rupp, 2003). ACs may include various types of information giving, testing techniques, and feedback formats (International Task Force on Assessment Center Guidelines, 2000; Thornton & Rupp, 2005). Although ACs have historically been used for managerial selection, promotion, and the diagnosis of training needs, with the resulting assessment being the end product of the process, they are gaining increasing popularity in industry as a way to structure behaviorally based training and development programs (Joiner, 2002). This shift from an assessment focus to a developmental focus has prompted the use of the term *developmental assessment center* (DAC) to refer to the use of the AC method for the purpose of employee development (Iles & Forster, 1994). A survey by Spychalski, Quiñones, Gaugler, and Pohley (1997) revealed that nearly 40% of the ACs being used in organizations are for the purpose of employee development.

One specific DAC model, developed by Thornton and Rupp (2005) and based on the work of others (Boehm, 1985; Carrick & Williams, 1999; Engelbrecht & Fischer, 1995; Goodge, 1991; Griffiths & Goodge, 1994; Jones & Whitmore, 1995; Lee, 2000, 2003; Lee & Beard, 1994; Povah, 1986), is illustrated in Figure 1 of Rupp, Snyder, Gibbons, and Thornton (this issue, p. 75). In this model, participants receive instruction on competencies and their meaning and soon after take part in a block of simulation exercises while being observed by trained assessors. Following this, employees reflect on their perceived strengths and weakness on the competencies and receive feedback that reflects the aggregate perceptions of the multiple observations taken by multiple assessors across multiple simulation exercises. Participants then have the opportunity to take part in a second block of exercises where they can put their received feedback into practice. They then receive additional developmental feedback at the end with a focus on improvement and ways in which the learning can be transferred back to the their work environment (Goodge, 1991).

In a DAC, feedback is not limited to the pass–fail feedback usually given following traditional assessments (Griffiths & Allen, 1987). For real developmental learning to occur, developmental feedback needs to be detailed, behaviorally specific, and high quality (Boehm, 1985; Francis-Smythe, & Smith, 1997), and it must provide participants with information about how to modify their behavior (Arnold, 1987). Participants are encouraged to take an active role in the feedback session, self-reflecting and discussing with the assessor ways in which proficiency on the competencies could be improved, in terms of the exercise scenarios and the participants' real-work environments (Cochran, Hinckle, & Dusenberry, 1987; Griffiths & Allen, 1987). In this situation, assessment and development are closely linked—

DACs attempt to change the behavior of participants in addition to measuring aspects of managerial performance (Howard, 1974; Jones & Whitmore, 1995; Klimoski & Brickner, 1987; Klimoski & Strickland, 1977). In fact, Hollenbeck (1990) suggested that it is this intervention quality of DACs that has led to their continued use in organizations.

USING DACS TO FOSTER WORKPLACE FAIRNESS

What has been discussed thus far is not novel. Indeed, this special issue is committed to the discussion of DAC interventions, the identification of competencies best suited for development via DAC programs, and methods for evaluating ACs used as training interventions. Thus, we refer readers to the other articles in this section for further detail on the general DAC method. In this article, we take a more specific focus: how DACs might be used to enable organizations to better meet their fairness and diversity management goals. Substantial literature shows a critical link between the degree to which employees perceive management as being fair and their subsequent attitudes and behaviors (Cohen-Charash & Spector, 2001; Colquitt, Conlon, Wesson, Porter, & Ng, 2001). In addition, recent research has indicated that managers can create a just climate for their subordinates that has an important impact on both individual and team performance (Liao & Rupp, 2005; Rupp, Bashshur, & Liao, in press). Indeed, employees who believe that management is fair are more satisfied, are more committed to the organization, are better performers, and are reported to engage in more citizenship behaviors at work than are those who believe otherwise about management. Conversely, when employees perceive injustice, they often retaliate in the form of counterproductive work behaviors, theft, sabotage, and lowered performance and attitudes. Therefore, in addition to developing managers on traditional performance competencies such as problem solving, information seeking, planning and organizing, communication, and so forth, it behooves the organization to consider how management might be coached to engage in practices that serve organizational interests and foster perceptions of fairness among employees. This article is based on two fundamental propositions:

> *Proposition 1.* Fairness is a construct that can be easily reconstituted as a behaviorally defined performance dimension or competency.

> *Proposition 2.* DACs are especially well suited for training managers to alter their behaviors so that they can be effective and fair.

In the sections that follow, we briefly review the literature on employee fairness, often referred to as *organizational justice.* We then present the well-established four-component model of employee justice—distributive, procedural, interpersonal, and interactional justice—and reformulate this work as four behavioral competencies to be developed in a DAC program. Finally, we discuss what such a program might look like.

WORKPLACE FAIRNESS

A great deal of research has been conducted in the area of organizational justice in the last decades (for a review, see Cropanzano, Byrne, Bobocel, & Rupp, 2001). Employees' perceptions of fairness are often based on the actions of their managers (Rupp & Cropanzano, 2002). The reason is that managers are often employees' most proximal organizational representatives. In addition, manager–subordinate interactions are frequent and commonly occur during processes such as performance appraisals, disciplinary proceedings, discussions about career planning and future opportunities, and other meetings where the subordinate can make judgments regarding fair treatment and processes. We also know from social identity theory and the group-value/relational model of justice (Lind, 1995; Lind & Tyler, 1988; Tyler, 1997; Tyler, Degoey, & Smith, 1996; Tyler & Lind, 1992; Tyler & Smith, 1998) that employees seek to be respected and appreciated within their working groups; thus, fair treatment coming from one's manager is relevant because it defines this important interpersonal tie. Indeed, research based on social exchange theory has shown that employees' perceptions of their managers shape their perceptions of other workplace factors (e.g., organizational support; Eisenberger, Stinglhamber, Vandenberghe, Sucharski, & Rhoades, 2002). The quality of the manager–employee exchange relationship is strongly dependent on employees' perceptions of managerial fairness. In fact, perceived fairness of managers has a stronger influence on employees' subsequent thoughts and actions than does fairness coming from other sources, such as the organization as a whole (Rupp & Cropanzano, 2002). Because such judgments are made based on the actions of managers, it follows that training managers to engage in fair actions will result in positive perceptions of fairness—and, consequently, positive attitudes and behaviors—from the employee. Consequently, the question becomes, might fairness be viewed not in terms of employee perceptions, as has been done in the past, but rather as a managerial competency that can be trained and developed?

Much of the research on organizational justice takes the perspective of the employees and studies their perceptions of how they are treated by their managers and organizations (Kray & Lind, 2002). Greenberg (1982, 1987) calls this a reactive approach to justice, because it is concerned with how employees react to a situation. We suggest taking a proactive approach. This involves determining how one creates situations that are perceived as being fair. A manager can proactively take measures to create circumstances that may lead his or her employees perceiving a situation or outcome as being fair. Conceptually, the two perspectives are linked: A manager is proactive in his or her actions to promote a particular reaction from his or her employees—namely, perceptions of fairness.

Greenberg and Wiethoff (2001) described a six-step generic framework for analyzing organizational justice: assessment, reaction, response feedback, creation, event feedback, and enactment (see Figure 1). The first two steps, assessment and reaction, represent the process studied by the majority of justice researchers, who take a reactive orientation. After assessment and reaction have occurred, the manager then recognizes the employee's reaction as a response to a perception of injustice (response feedback stage), prompting him or her to create a new approach or take new actions that may alleviate the current situation or prevent a similar response in another employee (creation stage). After evaluating the results of this new approach (event feedback stage), the manager may choose to enact the approach only in this particular case or might make the new approach a part of the organization's ongoing procedures (enactment stage). These latter three steps represent a proactive orientation and the approach on which this article is based. That is, this article focuses on catalyzing behavioral change among managers to positively affect employee performance and attitudes through heightened employee justice judgments.

A FOUR-COMPONENT FAIRNESS MODEL

Although justice is indeed a social construction, subjectively decided by those who observe or experience it (Degoey, 2000; Folger & Cropanzano, 1998), we argue

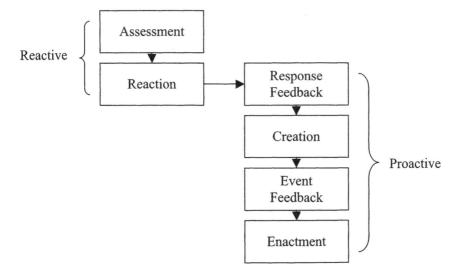

FIGURE 1   Greenberg and Wiethoff's (2001) framework of justice reactions.

that the theory and research in this area have advanced enough to define a set of generalizable managerial behaviors that are used by employees to make justice judgments. Research has shown that employees evaluate the fairness of four distinct yet interrelated classes of events (Colquitt, 2001). First, an outcome can be evaluated as being fair or unfair. This is called *distributive justice*. Second, the process by which an outcome or allocation decision is arrived at can be considered just or unjust. This is referred to as *procedural justice*. Third, *interpersonal justice* can be thought of as the quality of the interpersonal treatment of an individual when procedures are enacted. Finally, *informational justice* is the extent to which adequate information is provided about why procedures were used or outcomes distributed in a certain way (Colquitt et al., 2001).

Distributive Justice

Employees make fairness judgments about such outcomes as pay, opportunities for advancement, receiving (or not receiving) a promotion, and so on. Much of the research on distributive justice has been based on equity theory (Adams, 1965), which considers outcomes and the relative contributions of the recipient. A justice judgment is made about a particular outcome (e.g., a promotion) by evaluating one's inputs relative to the outcome and then by comparing this ratio to the input-to-outcome ratio of a referent other (someone who is similarly situated as the person making the judgment). One might consider tenure, performance, and loyalty as inputs and compare these to the tenure, performance, and loyalty of another who received the same promotion and thus make a fairness decision about the outcome based on this comparison. If a balanced comparison is found (e.g., the input-to-outcome ratio is the same for both individuals), then the outcome is considered fair. However, if the employee finds that the ratio of inputs to outcomes is different than that of the referent other (e.g., one individual receiving a promotion finds that his or her level of tenure, performance, and loyalty is much greater than that of another who received a promotion), then injustice is perceived. Another well-accepted notion regarding distributive justice is that justice is perceived when an outcome reflects one's efforts at work, is appropriate to the work that one has completed, reflects what one has contributed to the organization, and is justified given one's performance (Leventhal, 1976).

This research has implications for what managerial actions might help define distributive justice as a managerial competency. Specifically, by ensuring that outcomes are relevant to an employee's work, accurately reflect the employee's efforts at work, and are reasonable given the employee's performance level and contribution to the organization, a manager may be able to ensure that employees will view their outcomes relative to their efforts as being fair. In addition, applying the same standard for decision making can help ensure equity among allocations. Last, managers may influence their subordinates' distributive justice perceptions by en-

TABLE 1
Distributive Justice as a Managerial Behavioral Competency

Providing outcomes that reflect employees' efforts
Providing outcomes to employees that are appropriate given their work
Providing outcomes that reflect the contribution employees have made or are making to the organization
Providing outcomes that are reasonable in light of employees' performance
Providing an appropriate amount of information about the efforts and outcomes of others (for the purpose of making more accurate comparisons)

---

suring that subordinates are making accurate comparisons. That is, the accuracy of employees' justice judgments will be hindered if they are not comparing themselves to an appropriate referent. They might misperceive the amount of effort put forth by their comparison other or misinterpret that person's outcomes. Managers can further ensure that their subordinates make appropriate comparisons by making public what people are doing, the extent to which they are achieving their goals, and, if appropriate, how they are being recognized for their efforts. Some outcome information, such as pay and raises, may be naturally kept private in some organizations, but information about individual projects, goals, progress toward goals, and outcomes such as promotions can certainly be made public and allow for accurate input-to-outcome comparisons. We also know from the goal-setting literature that such strategies can influence employee motivation and performance as well (Locke & Latham, 2002). Table 1 lists specific managerial behaviors that may affect subordinates' perceptions of distributive justice.

Procedural Justice

Processes and procedures used to arrive at an outcome can be evaluated as fair or unfair. Two criteria are relevant to procedural justice perceptions: process control (the opportunity to voice an opinion and point of view) and decision control (the ability to influence the outcome of the proceedings; Thibaut & Walker, 1975). The presence of decision control positively affects the participants' perceptions of justice. Likewise, in the absence of decision control, having the opportunity to express oneself (i.e., having "voice") leads to perceptions of fairness (Folger, 1977).

This effect has clear relevance for workplace behavior. When a manager is involved in a decision-making process, an employee may be more likely to perceive the outcome as being fair when he or she is allowed some decision control. Because decision control involves giving the employee the ability to influence the outcome directly, a better term for decision control may be *choice*. When an employee is given the ability to choose the outcome, his or her perception of fairness will be greater. Behaviorally speaking, a manager could influence perceptions of justice by allowing employees some degree of choice in decision-making processes. For example, imagine a case in which a manager must inform an employee that he or she must put in 10 hr of overtime this week to complete a project with a looming deadline. In this case, the outcome will be the employee's working 10 extra hr. Now imagine that the manager offers the employee the choice between coming to work 2 hr early every day, staying 2 hr late every day, or coming in early and staying late 1 hr each day. In each case, the outcome is the same (10 extra hr), but the employee is now given decision control in that the manager does not choose for him or her how and when to put in the extra hours. The outcome will more likely be perceived as being fair when the employee is given this choice than when no choice is offered.

In addition, when decision control cannot be offered, the manager has the ability to increase perceptions of fairness by offering the employee the ability to express himself or herself to the decision maker before the outcome is determined. So this time, imagine that a manager has to inform his or her employees that they must all (as a group) attend an after-hours training session. The session can take place either before or after normal working hours but not during. The manager must decide whether to schedule the training before or after hours, knowing that some employees would prefer before, some after. If the manager arbitrarily makes the decision, some employees are likely to consider the outcome as being unfair. However, if the manager offers the employees the opportunity to express to him or her their preferred time and the reason why they prefer it, the employees will be granted the opportunity to affect the decision indirectly through voice and will likely perceive the outcome as being more fair than if they had no voice.

Empirical studies on the effects of voice and decision control are abundant, and the findings are well-accepted among organizational justice researchers (e.g., Brockner et al., 2001; Folger, 1977; Korsgaard & Roberson, 1995; Lind, Kanfer, & Earley, 1990; Lind, Kray, & Thompson, 1998; McFarlin & Sweeney, 1996; Tyler, Rasinski, & Spodick, 1985; van den Bos & van Prooijen, 2001). Indeed, we know that giving employees voice increases their perceptions of procedural justice, for two reasons. First, having voice fosters perceptions of an increased chance of an outcome favorable to the employee. This is a self-seeking and instrumental reason. However, there is a second reason, which is symbolic. That is, employees who are given voice may feel valued and may therefore be accepting of an unfavorable outcome. This is evidenced by research that shows that even postdecision voice can increase procedural justice perceptions (Lind et al., 1990). What has not been tested empirically to a great extent is whether managers can learn to change their behaviors to provide employees with increased voice and whether such training leads to heightened employee procedural justice perceptions. Also needing empirical investigation is how managers can be trained in responding to the concerns voiced by employees. That is, can they effectively do something about employee concerns, and can such compromises lead to a significant increase in employee procedural justice perceptions above and beyond the effects of voice alone (without follow-through)?

The justice literature has provided six criteria for a fair process (Leventhal, 1980). That is, for a process to be considered fair, it has to be consistent (i.e., the process must be consistently applied to all persons and over time), free of bias (i.e., the decision maker must take a neutral stance, with no bias given to one party or option over the other), accurate (i.e., procedures must be based on accurate information), correctable (i.e., the process must be able to be appealed, and a process must exist to reverse bad decisions), representative (i.e., all the various interests affected by the process must be taken into account), and ethical (i.e., the process must follow prevalent moral and ethical standards).

From the standpoint of a manager, these rules are easily translated into behaviors or actions. When implementing a procedure, perceptions of fairness are greatest when the manager (a) is careful to apply the procedure consistently to all employees over time, (b) remains neutral and does not favor one person or group over another, (c) gathers accurate information and uses it to implement the procedure, (d) allows an appeal process for all decisions and makes the effort to follow such process to reverse a "bad" decision, (e) ensures that all interests are taken into account when designing and implementing a procedure, and (f) determines and adheres to the prevailing standard of ethics for the organization or group. According to Leventhal's model (1980), a manager meeting these behavioral criteria when implementing procedures will increase his or her employees' judgments of procedural justice, which will lead to positive attitudes and behaviors among employees. The question that remains is whether managers can be trained to exhibit such an array of behaviors.

Although several prominent theories (e.g., Leventhal, 1980; Thibaut & Walker, 1975) address processes themselves, Lind and Tyler (1988) developed a model that explained why process was so important to people. In their relational model, they argued that procedures are important to fairness because they relate information to the employee about his or her place in the collective. The authors suggested that the procedure is not as important as the impact that the procedure has on one's relationship with the authority figure or organization that implements the process. An unfair process is one that threatens the individual's sense of identity within the group. Tyler and Lind (1992) defined three relational factors that are critical to this identity-building process: trust, neutrality, and standing. Trust refers specifically to an individual's trust in an authority figure, generated by an earnest effort by the authority figure to "do the right thing" and the individual's perception of benevolence and honesty in the authority figure (Folger & Cropanzano, 1998). Neutrality refers to remaining free from bias, being honest, and making decisions based on fact (Tyler & Lind, 1992). Standing involves recognizing and upholding the rights of others as human beings (Folger & Cropanzano, 1998) or as members of a group, organization, institution, society, or state (Lind & Tyler, 1988).

TABLE 2
Procedural Justice as a Managerial Behavioral Competency

Carefully applying procedures consistently to all employees

Remaining neutral and not showing favoritism

Showing trustworthiness by conveying that actions are motivated by kindness, integrity, and genuine concern for the needs of others

Gathering accurate information and using it to implement procedures

Allowing for an appeal process for all decisions, allowing for bad decisions to be appealed and reversed

Taking all employees' interests into account when implementing a procedure

Communicating information accurately to employees

Providing explanations to employees for decisions and procedures

Providing employees some degree of control over decisions and procedures

Providing employees voice (the opportunity to express their opinion about decisions and processes)

Responding to employees' voiced concerns in some way

Recognizing employees' status by treating them with dignity, decency, and respect for the rights that are owed to each employee

---

Behavioral expressions of neutrality are discussed in the context of Leventhal's criteria (1980), but trust can also be described in terms of managerial actions. First, an employee's perception of managerial trustworthiness is influenced by five factors: consistency, integrity, sharing and delegation of control, communication (accuracy, explanations, and openness), and demonstration of concern (Whitener, Brodt, Korsgaard, & Werner, 1998). A manager may increase employee trust by displaying consistent behaviors, being honest, providing others with control, communicating information accurately, providing explanations to others, being open to communication with others, and showing concern for the welfare of others. Lind and Tyler's model suggests that in establishing trust, a manager will increase procedural fairness perceptions from his or her employees and consequently reap the benefits that such perceptions create (e.g., employee citizenship behaviors, commitment, employee retention). Table 2 lists the managerial behaviors that can be derived from Leventhal's criteria and the relational model.

Interactional Justice: Informational and Interpersonal Justice

Interactional justice, which includes the subfacets of informational and interpersonal justice, deals with how an individual is treated during the implementation of procedures (Bies & Moag, 1986). Four interpersonal variables affect employees' perceptions of justice: justification, truthfulness, respect, and propriety. The former two characterize informational justice, and the latter two central on interpersonal justice. Justification involves providing information after an injustice has occurred, and it serves to reduce perceptions of unfairness. Justifications often take the form of explanations and apologies (Bies, 1987). Truthfulness involves being honest but also being candid. Research has shown that people want to be told the truth in a forthright, realistic, and accurate way (Bies, 1987). Respect refers to courteous, noninsulting, noncritical treatment. Propriety of remarks, questions, or other communication involves the nature of the communication. Asking inappropriately personal questions or making prejudicial statements reflects a lack of propriety.

Interactionally fair managerial behavior should involve (a) providing explanations or apologies after an injustice has occurred, (b) being honest and forthright, (c) providing information that is realistic and accurate, (d) being courteous, (e) refraining from insults and overly critical treatment, (f) communicating in ways that avoid prejudicial overtones, and (g) avoiding questions or remarks regarding others' personal information.

Other research has presented seven managerial responsibilities for ensuring fairness in decision making (Folger & Bies, 1989). This taxonomy, in behavioral terms, includes giving consideration to others' viewpoints, suppressing biases, being consistent in the application of decision-making criteria, giving timely feedback after a decision, expressing honesty, and treating others with courtesy and civility. Although some of these elements are similar to elements of procedural justice, the importance of the procedural and interactional elements is clear in the Folger and Bies taxonomy, as are the different emphases of the two subelements, informational and interpersonal justice.

We can deduce several managerial behaviors based on this research that are indicative of interpersonal and informational justice (see Table 3).

TRAINING FOR JUSTICE

In the previous section, we seek to reconceptualize justice as managerial competency, defined behaviorally, such that organizations might be able to design training programs to develop managers on the fairness construct. Such development can serve to increase employee perceptions of fairness and, as a result, improve employees' workplace attitudes and performance. A paucity of research exists that focuses on fairness training. Though there is some tangentially related research in areas that have touched on issues related to justice, such as impression management and interpersonal skills development, training managerial fairness is an area that has received little empirical examination. A few notable studies do, however, provide a promising start to the exploration of this concept.

First, Skarlicki and Latham (1996) applied Leventhal's principles (1980) of procedural justice in developing a training intervention for a group of union leaders. The researchers' goal was to increase fairness perceptions among the union members whose leaders underwent the justice training. In addition, they hypothe-

TABLE 3
Interactional Justice as a Managerial Behavioral Competency

Interpersonal justice
    Communicating with employees in ways that avoid prejudicial overtones
    Avoiding questions or remarks regarding employees' personal information
    Giving consideration to employees' viewpoints
    Showing respect for employees' rights and opinions
    Defining and adhering to ethical standards
    Remaining courteous to all employees
    Refraining from insults and overly critical treatment of employees
    Showing concern for employees' welfare
    Treating employees with dignity
Informational justice
    Providing employees with timely feedback after making a decision
    Being honest with employees
    Using open communication with employees
    Providing explanations and (if appropriate) apologies to employees following an injustice
    Being forthright in communications with employees
    Providing employees realistic and accurate information

---

sized that, due to the increase in fairness perceptions, the union members would engage in more organizational citizenship behaviors toward the union. The union leaders underwent a training program that was designed to increase their awareness of and provide strategies for developing fair treatment through increased consistency, bias suppression, accuracy, correctability, voice, and ethicality (Leventhal's procedural justice rules). Issues related to each of these principles were discussed, often using case examples from within the union itself, and strategies were devised to implement behavior that followed these principles. The training program also used role-play exercises and real-life practice to teach the behaviors necessary to improve fairness.

Using pre- and posttest measures of fairness perceptions, the authors showed that the justice training increased union members' perceptions of their leaders' interactional and procedural fairness. In addition, they found that union members displayed more organizational citizenship behaviors toward the union after their leaders' participation in the justice training program. The findings were then successfully replicated in a second union group (Skarlicki & Latham, 1997). In this study, the authors measured organizational citizenship behaviors directed at the organization and organizational citizenship behaviors directed at other union members. Results showed that both types of citizenship were more prevalent among union workers whose leaders had undergone justice training.

Similarly, Cole and Latham (1997) designed a training program that focused on aspects of procedural justice as it related to disciplinary processes. This program focused on six factors that had been found to be related to fairness in disciplinary action (Ball, 1991): an explanation of the performance problem being addressed, the supervisor's demeanor, subordinate's process control, employee counseling, arbitrariness, and privacy. The format of the training consisted of lectures, group discussions, and role-plays. During these activities, each of the six factors was discussed or illustrated, and the participants were given the chance to practice applying the principles and giving and receiving feedback. After the instruction was complete, the participants were videotaped while performing a simulated disciplinary proceeding with a union employee. Union members then assessed the proceedings (as did subject matter experts), and perceptions of fairness were measured. The authors discovered that the union members and the subject matter experts found the disciplinary proceedings performed by managers who had received training to be more fair than the proceedings by those who did not receive any justice training. Additionally, the researchers found that the managers who underwent training had higher self-efficacy and higher outcome expectancies regarding the administration of disciplinary action than did the managers who did not receive training.

These studies show support for the idea that justice can be trained as a skill and that organizations benefit from this training through high levels of organizational citizenship behaviors displayed by the subordinates whose perceptions of justice regarding their supervisors increase as a result of this kind of training. However, there remains a need to flesh out the complexities of how all justice principles can be incorporated into training programs and of what outcomes can and should be measured to assess the effectiveness of such training. We seek to expand this research in three important ways. First, we considered four justice subcompetencies and defined them behaviorally, whereas past research has sought to develop only procedural or interactional justice. Second, we propose that DACs are an ideal format for developing managerial justice. Cole and Latham (1997) selected their training format (lectures, group discussions, role-plays) based on findings that posit that such a format results in a relatively permanent change in on-the-job behavior (Burke & Day, 1986). Skarlicki and Latham (1996, 1997) selected their format (discussion, group discussion, role-plays) based on methods that were reported in past research to be effective. DACs incorporate both of the methods used in these studies, as well as other methods designed to maximize learning and training transfer.

WHY DACS OVER OTHER FORMS OF TRAINING?

We are certainly not arguing in this article that DACs are the only way in which fairness among managers might be fostered. Indeed, at the start of the article, we mention several different training techniques that have proven effective for developing certain competencies in certain domains (Arthur, Bennett, Edens, & Bell,

2003). What we do argue is that the DAC design offers several qualities that are likely to maximize training effectiveness.

One of the features that make DACs a particularly effective training tool is the job-related simulation exercise. Not only do the simulation exercises used in DACs elicit relevant behaviors that can be observed and evaluated, but the exercises themselves provide the opportunity for experiential learning, practice, self-reflection, and performance improvement. By using simulation exercises, DACs offer a training environment in which objective assessments of job-relevant behaviors can be made (Goodge, 1991). The simulation exercises can (and should) be specifically designed to be similar to those situations encountered in the manager's worklife. This replication ensures that the resulting assessment will serve as an accurate representation of the manager's strengths and weaknesses in relation to the actual circumstances of his or her job and organization. Making the simulation exercises highly relevant to the manager's job has the added benefit of ensuring internalization of the behaviors and skills learned through the AC process. In fact, Schmitt, Ford, and Stults (1986) found that participants in an AC showed significant change in their perceptions of their own abilities on several dimensions before and after the exercises, even without the benefit of feedback.

Further, the use of simulation exercises allows participants the chance to practice and experiment with new behaviors that they might not necessarily feel comfortable with when on the job (Thornton & Cleveland, 1990) and to do so in a context that is similar to the actual job environment. Because of the fidelity of the training environment and content to the "real world," transfer of training using a DAC is maximized. This kind of utilization of active participation in the training process, which is crucial to adult learning (Mehta, 1978), helps to make apparent the benefits of the DAC process to the trainees themselves.

A third benefit of simulation exercises is that they provide learning opportunities through behavioral modeling (Bandura, 1986). Participation in exercises with other managers who are performing on the same dimensions allows a trainee to observe the actions of others and model their successful behaviors. For example, Smith-Jentsch, Salas, and Baker (1996) found that, when compared to other training formats (i.e., lecture and lecture plus demonstration), a format similar to an AC approach (i.e., behavioral modeling that focused on role-playing combined with performance feedback) improved learning of assertiveness skills.

A second key feature of DACs is that the feedback sessions form a much larger portion of the time involved in the center than that found in a traditional assessment-focused center. Rather than merely informing the participant of his or her strengths and weaknesses, DAC feedback sessions involve discussing ways to improve. In most training settings, providing participants with knowledge of the effectiveness of their efforts is essential for performance improvement (Kluger & DeNisi, 1996). Providing specific feedback about why a negative (or positive) assessment was made and how a deficiency can be corrected can allow the participant to learn how to correct his or her behavior and may even provide intrinsic motivation by making the tasks personally relevant. Feedback in the context of a DAC meets these criteria. However, the feedback must be detailed, behaviorally specific, and of high quality for real developmental learning to occur (Boehm, 1985; Francis-Smythe & Smith, 1997).

Another benefit of DACs is that the results of the feedback session are used to create a training/development action plan—based on quantitative data (dimension ratings) and qualitative data (assessor comments and feedback)—that can be implemented on the job (Engelbrecht & Fischer, 1995). Because the AC process requires specificity in regard to the desired behaviors for each skill or dimension, a developmental action plan provides information on (a) specific dimensions that require development and (b) specific behaviors that the participant can learn to improve these dimensions. In this way, the assessment aspect of the center drives the development aspect and allows the feedback session to serve as a training component. Finally, the development plan incorporates ways to ensure the transfer of the knowledge and skills learned in the training session into the participant's job.

SPECIFICS OF A FAIRNESS DAC PROGRAM

Some methods are more effective than others, depending on the type and content of the material being taught. A justice training program requires a variety of components (see Table 4). Managers must come to understand what fairness is and what costs and benefits are associated with their fair or unfair behaviors. Managers must also be instructed in what specific behaviors are perceived as being fair or unfair by their subordinates. They then need some sort of practice using these behaviors; they need to be assessed in some way; and they need to receive feedback on how their behaviors were perceived and if they match the behavioral criteria specified. Finally, goals should be set or an action plan formed to maximize transfer of training. Each of these components is best carried out using a different training format,

TABLE 4
Necessary Components of a Justice Training Program

Instruction on the principles, theories, and research surrounding organizational justice
Illustration of the costs associated with perceived injustice, and the benefits of perceived justice
Training on the managerial behaviors that elicit distributive, procedural, and interactional fairness
    perceptions among employees
Opportunities for the managers to practice these behaviors
Assessment of managers' fairness-related performance during these practice sessions
Provision of feedback on the managers' fairness-related performance
Development of action plans for transferring the knowledge gleaned from the training program into
    the managers' working lives

such as instruction, simulation exercises, assessment, and developmental feedback. As mentioned, a DAC framework allows training developers a structure to incorporate all of these components into a single program.

Steps in Developing a Justice DAC

Table 5 lists the necessary steps in the development of a managerial fairness DAC program. It is important to note that the relevant dimensions—in this case, the subdimensions of justice—should inform the development of each step in the process. Although explicit detail regarding each of these steps is beyond the scope of this article, we encourage interested readers to consult the practitioner-oriented texts available that provide detailed instruction in developing simulation exercises (e.g., Thornton & Mueller-Hanson, 2004), assessor training programs, and DAC evaluation protocols (e.g., Thornton & Rupp, 2005). The various models put forth in these texts provide the framework for the process model described in this article.

The first step involves conducting an analysis of the work context. Critical incidents illustrating situations involving fair and unfair actions on the part of management can be collected from employees and managers. This material can then be used to develop simulation exercises that challenge and assess DAC participants. It is important that the simulation exercises be high in fidelity while at the same time sufficiently removed from actual situations or events such that they avoid generating controversy.

Once the simulation exercises are developed, behaviorally anchored rating scales (BARS; Smith & Kendall, 1963) can be designed to aid assessors in rating the participants on the justice competencies. Figure 2 illustrates an example of such a rating scale. As shown, sample behaviors are provided at various points on the rating scale to aid assessors in making appropriate competency ratings. These behavioral anchors can be gleaned from the critical incidents collected previously or from pilot tests of the exercises. This particular ordering of steps ensures that the BARS reflect the behaviors that are most likely to be demonstrated in the corresponding exercise. The behavioral anchors used in each BARS should be clear and

TABLE 5
Steps in Developing a Justice Development Assessment Center
(DAC) Program

Collect critical incidents
Develop simulation exercises
Develop behaviorally anchored rating scales (BARS)
Pilot-test and videorecord
Train assessors
Implement developmental assessment center (DAC)
Evaluate the effectiveness of the program

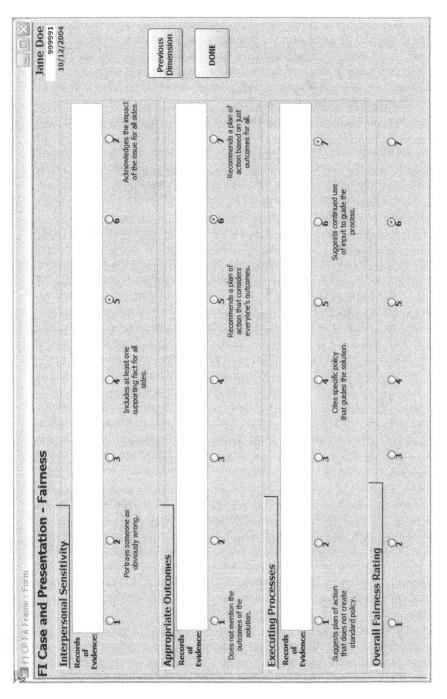

FIGURE 2   An example of a behaviorally anchored rating scale (BARS) from a managerial fairness developmental assessment center (DAC) program.

specific and rooted within the context of the exercise. It is important to note that a separate BARS should be created for each exercise so that anchors reflect behaviors likely to be seen in each particular simulated situation. In addition, BARS should be continually monitored for quality, and the behavioral anchors continually improved on, as the DAC staff comes to learn about the behaviors commonly manifested within the simulation exercises.

The next step required is pilot-testing the simulation exercises. Not only does this test allow the DAC developer to determine the appropriateness of the exercise content, the difficulty level, and the degree to which exercises elicit observable justice-related behaviors, but it can also generate materials (e.g., video clips) useful for assessor training and the classroom instruction component of the DAC program. If major adjustments are made to the exercises or BARS as a result of pilot-testing, additional pilot-testing may be needed.

Before the managerial fairness DAC program can be implemented, assessors must be thoroughly trained and interrater reliability must be established to ensure accurate assessment (and, consequently, accurate feedback). In the assessor training programs that we have conducted for the purpose of justice-focused DACs, we have first put the assessors through the DAC program as if they were participants. This is an effective method because it allows them to be heavily exposed to the program materials and the challenges faced by participants. We have also conducted a series of written tests on both the justice competency definitions and the exercise content. The assessors then take part in two essential components of any AC assessor training program (see Schleicher, Day, Mayes, & Riggio, 2002; Thornton & Rupp, 2003, 2005): first, process training, in which they are trained in systematically observing, recording, classifying, and rating the behaviors displayed in the exercises; and, second, frame-of-reference training, which involves using video recordings of exercises to practice making ratings and calibrating judgments across assessors until all assessors share a common frame of reference. Assessors must also be trained in integrating their ratings and in developing and delivering feedback reports.

Once the quality of the exercises and rating materials is established and the competence of assessors certified, the managerial fairness DAC can be implemented. The effectiveness of the program, both to assess managers' competency on the justice dimensions and to foster positive change in their fairness-related behaviors (without compromising their performance on other competencies), should be continually monitored. Rupp, Gibbons, et al. (this issue, p. 171) describe many pieces of evidence that can (and should) be marshaled to support DAC program effectiveness. These include (a) assessing the appropriateness of the content; (b) looking at the internal structure of the ratings; (c) assessing change in proficiency on the dimensions over time; and (d) considering participant reactions, engagement, learning, and participation in subsequent development activities. In the case of a managerial fairness DAC, the ultimate litmus test of the program's effectiveness lies in whether a positive change occurred in the perceptions of fairness made by the managers' subordinates, which we illustrate in the following section.

An Illustrative Case Study

Figure 3 illustrates what a managerial fairness DAC might look like. We have conducted programs similar to this one in organizations where fairness perceptions among employees were declining. Compared to those of a control group, managers who attended the DAC showed no significant decline in fairness judgments, suggesting that the DAC intervention may have been successful in this "sinking ship" type of situation (Baldwin, Rupp, & Bashshur, 2005). Future research is certainly needed to further flesh out these issues.

As shown in Figure 3, before participants attend the DAC, baseline measures are collected regarding employees' perceptions of their manager's (i.e., the DAC participant's) level of distributive, procedural, and interactional justice. Several measures are available for this purpose in the justice literature (e.g., see Colquitt, 2001). The first component of training involves more traditional classroom instruction. Participants are presented with information regarding the meaning of the competencies and their behavioral manifestations. This can be supplemented with video clips of other managers (actors) displaying effective and ineffective fairness behaviors. To ensure comprehension, participants can also be required to pass written quizzes on the meaning of the fairness competencies.

After the fairness competencies have become completely transparent, the participants then engage in a block of simulation exercises. As shown in the figure, such exercises might include, for example, a role-play in which the manager has to resolve conflict between employees, a leaderless group discussion in which a group of managers must decide on a strategy for redistributing the budget, and a case study–analysis exercise in which the manager must develop and present a plan for implementing a reduction in force. This aspect of the program is extraordinarily active and often stressful. Therefore, time is allowed following the block of exercises for the managers to rest and reflect on their own competence on the fairness dimensions.

Each manager is then given feedback on his or her performance in the first block of exercises, and the manager and assessor work together to develop some short-term goals for improving the manager's fairness in the second block of exercises. In the DAC illustrated in the figure, these exercises include an in-box task in which the manager must shuffle through a plethora of employee complaints, a role-play in which the manager must carry out a sexual harassment investigation, and a case study–oral presentation task in which the manager presents decisions regarding the scheduling of vacation time to his or her staff. Following this second block of exercises, the manager is again given time for self-reflection. During these reflection times, the assessors are behind the scenes efficiently combining their ob-

Baseline measure: Employees' perceptions of distributive, procedural, and interactional justice

Classroom instruction
    -    Training on competencies
    -    Video clips
    -    Written quizzes

Block of simulation exercises, for example....
    -    Role-play of managing conflict between employees
    -    Leaderless group discussion about the redistribution of the budget
    -    Case study analysis and presentation for the purpose of developing a downsizing strategy

Self-reflection

Feedback and short term goal setting

Block of simulation exercises, for example....
    -    Inbox focused on incoming employee complaints
    -    Role play surrounding a sexual harassment investigation
    -    Case study analysis and presentation focused on the allocation of summer vacation time off

Self-reflection

Feedback on improvement from first block, goal setting, transfer of training

Program evaluation
    -    Participant reactions
    -    Time 2 measure of employee (subordinate) perceptions of distributive, procedural, and interactional justice
    -    Reassessment on same or parallel blocks of exercises

FIGURE 3   An example of a managerial fairness developmental assessment center (DAC) program.

servations of the candidates, coming to consensus regarding each participant's proficiency on the fairness competencies, and developing feedback reports. The program ends with a final feedback session in which (a) the assessor reports on the improvement observed from the first block of exercises to the second, (b) formal goals are set with regard to the manager's particular role in the organization, and (c) transfer of training is maximized by teaching the manager to generalize what was learned in the DAC to his or her actual work life.

As for any training intervention, it is crucial to evaluate the effectiveness of the program both in assessing the manager's true level of fairness and in fostering improvement over time. DAC program staff might consider collecting program reaction data from participants or taking a second measure of subordinates' perceptions of their manager's fairness some time following the training. More sophisticated evaluation can be made possible if fairness perceptions can be collected not only from subordinates of managers going through the DAC program but also from a control group who does not receive the training. Additionally, participants can be put back through the same or different blocks of exercises some time later, and improvement can again be assessed.

Balancing Fairness With Other Competencies

We alluded to the need for an organization's fairness goals to be balanced with its other goals involving managerial effectiveness. Being perceived as fair is certainly not the only competency that a manager is expected to possess. A program such as this should stress effective fairness. Training and development staff may therefore wish to embed fairness training into larger programs focused on general managerial competence (see Rupp, Gibbons, et al., this issue, p. 171). However, research has yet to be conducted that compares the effectiveness of programs focused on developing one competency (or a subset of competencies) to that of programs focused on developing a whole taxonomy of competencies or those targeted at managerial effectiveness overall. We think that when there is a strong need to develop competence in one particular area, a focused strategy may be best.

SUMMARY AND CONCLUSION

This article is based on two fundamental propositions. Our first proposition is that distributive, procedural, and interactional (i.e., interpersonal and informational) justice can be reconceptualized into behavioral competencies on which managers can be trained. We reviewed the justice literature and identified several sets of justice criteria from which just managerial behaviors can be defined. In the process, we hoped to convey to the psychologist-manager community that fairness, in addition to being a valuable goal for its own sake, can be used to the strategic advantage of the organization in that a workforce that collectively believes that it is treated fairly by management is apt to be happier, healthier, more committed, and harder working than one that believes otherwise (Colquitt et al., 2001; Liao & Rupp, 2005).

Our second proposition is that DACs are well suited for developing managers on these fairness competencies. DACs combine the advantages of a variety of training methods, allow for active experiential learning, focus on self-reflection, provide high-quality feedback, and offer multiple opportunities for participants to improve themselves within the course of the program. High-stakes situations involving conflict can be simulated in a safe environment, and managers can spend time away from work deliberating on the effect that their actions have on their subordinates.

It is important to note that a managerial fairness DAC such as that outlined in this article will cost the organization time and resources to develop and maintain. Critical incidents must be collected to inspire exercise content; exercises must be developed; assessors must be trained; and pilot and validation evidence must be collected. In addition, operating the DAC will require substantial time commitments on the part of the manager and participants, as well as the DAC staff. The duration of DAC programs ranges from a few hours to multiple days, depending on the complexity of the program. Whereas simpler versions of the DAC model presented in Figure 3 can certainly be used, DAC designers must balance time and cost with quality and developmental need. For example, only one block of simulation exercises might be used, though it will not allow participants the opportunity to respond to their feedback within the program. If the level of fairness displayed in the first block of exercises is generally high, further practice might not be necessary; but if the fair behaviors are unfamiliar and difficult for participants, the benefit of additional practice could justify the additional time and cost.

The field of organizational justice has enjoyed a long, rich history, resulting in many significant findings regarding the effects of employee justice perceptions. Similarly, the wealth of extant AC research—as well as continuing research into new applications of the AC method, including the use of DACs to foster learning and development—offers much value to managerial research and practice. The introduction of the DAC method as an applied vehicle for fostering workplace fairness offers a unique opportunity to mix the best of the applied and theoretical worlds of organizational justice and ACs. By defining fairness as a behavioral competency and illustrating how this dimension can be trained, we are proposing a new approach to both fields of research. Future research is clearly needed that empirically tests this unique approach. Such research will be beneficial to the fields of organizational justice, training, and DACs alike.

ACKNOWLEDGMENTS

This research was supported by a grant from the University of Illinois Campus Research Board.

We thank Alyssa Mitchell Gibbons and Sarah Janssen for their assistance on this project.

REFERENCES

Adams, J. S. (1965). Inequity in social exchange. In L. Berkowitz (Ed.), *Advances in experimental social psychology* (Vol. 2, pp. 267–299). New York: Academic Press.

Arnold, G. T. (1987). Feedback and career development. In H. W. More & R. C. Unsinger (Eds.), *The police assessment center.* Springfield, IL: Charles C. Thomas.

Arthur, W., Jr., Bennett, W., Jr., Edens, P. S., & Bell, S. T. (2003). Effectiveness of training in organizations: A meta-analysis of design and evaluation features. *Journal of Applied Psychology, 88,* 234–245.

Baldwin, A. M., Rupp, D. E., & Bashshur, M. R. (2005, April). *Managerial justice training: An application of developmental assessment centers.* Theoretical advancement presented at the 20th annual conference for the Society for Industrial and Organizational Psychology, Los Angeles, California.

Ball, G. A. (1991). *Outcomes of punishment incidents: The roles of subordinate perceptions, individual differences, and leader behavior.* Unpublished doctoral dissertation, Pennsylvania State University.

Bandura, A. (1986). *Social foundations of thought and action.* Englewood Cliffs, NJ: Prentice-Hall, Inc.

Bies, R. J., (1987). Beyond "voice": The influence of decision-maker justification and sincerity of procedural fairness judgments. *Representative Research in Social Psychology, 17,* 3–17.

Bies, R. J., & Moag, J. F. (1986). Interactional Justice: Communication criteria of fairness. In R. J. Lewicki, B. H. Sheppard, & M. H. Bazerman (Eds.), *Research on negotiations in organizations* (Vol. 1, pp. 43–55). Greenwich, CT: JAI Press.

Boehm, V. R. (1985). Using assessment centers for management development—Five applications. *Journal of Management Development, 4*(4), 40–51.

Brockner, J., Ackerman, G., Greenberg, J., Gelfand, M. J., Francesco, A. M., Chen, Z. X., et al. (2001). Culture and procedural justice: The influence of power distance on reactions to voice. *Journal of Experimental Social Psychology, 37,* 300–315.

Burke, M. J., & Day, R. R. (1986). A cumulative study of the effectiveness of managerial training. *Journal of Applied Psychology, 71,* 232–246.

Campbell, J. P., & Kuncel, N. R. (2001). Individual and team training. In N. Anderson, D. Ones, H. Sinangil, & C. Viswesvaran (Eds.), *Handbook of industrial, work, and organizational psychology* (Vol. 1, pp. 278–312). Thousand Oaks, CA: Sage.

Carrick, P., & Williams, R. (1999). Developmental centers: A review of assumptions. *Human Resource Management Review, 9,* 77–91.

Cochran, D. S., Hinckle, T. W., & Dusenberry, D. (1987). Designing a developmental assessment center in a government agency: A case study. *Public Personnel Management, 16,* 145–152.

Cohen-Charash, Y., & Spector, P. E. (2001). The role of justice in organizations: A meta-analysis. *Organizational Behavior and Human Decision Processes, 86,* 278–321.

Cole, N. D., & Latham, G. P. (1997). Effects of training in procedural justice on perceptions of disciplinary fairness by unionized employees and disciplinary subject matter experts. *Journal of Applied Psychology, 82,* 699–705.

Colquitt, J. A. (2001). On the dimensionality of organizational justice: A construct validation of a measure. *Journal of Applied Psychology, 86,* 386–400.

Colquitt, J. A., Conlon, D. E., Wesson, M. J., Porter, C. O. L. H., & Ng, K. Y. (2001). Justice at the millennium: A meta-analytic review of 25 years of organizational justice research. *Journal of Applied Psychology, 86,* 425–445.

Cropanzano, R., Byrne, Z. S., Bobocel, D. R., & Rupp, D. E. (2001). Moral virtues, fairness heuristics, social entities, and other denizens of organizational justice. *Journal of Vocational Behavior, 58,* 164–209.

Degoey, P. (2000). Contagious justice: Exploring the social construction of justice in organizations. *Research in Organizational Behavior, 22,* 51–102.

Eisenberger, R., Stinglhamber, F., Vandenberghe, C., Sucharski, I. L., & Rhoades, L. (2002). Perceived supervisor support: Contributions to perceived organizational support. *Journal of Applied Psychology, 87,* 565–573.

Engelbrecht, A. S., & Fischer, A. H. (1995). The managerial performance implications of a developmental assessment center process. *Human Relations, 48*, 387–404.

Folger, R. (1977). Distributive and procedural justice: Combined impact of "voice" and improvement on experienced inequity. *Journal of Personality and Social Psychology, 35*, 108–119.

Folger, R., & Bies, R. J. (1989). Managerial responsibilities and procedural justice. *Employee Responsibilities and Rights Journal, 2*, 79–89.

Folger, R., & Cropanzano, R. (1998). *Organizational justice and human resource management.* Thousand Oaks, CA: Sage.

Francis-Smythe, J., & Smith, P. M. (1997). The psychological impact of assessment in a development center. *Human Relations, 50*, 149–167.

Goodge, P. (1991). Development centres: Guidelines for decision makers. *Journal of Management Development, 10*(3), 4–12.

Greenberg, J. (1982). Approaching equity and avoiding inequity in groups and organizations. In J. Greenberg & R. L. Cohen (Eds.), *Equity and justice in social behavior* (pp. 389–435). New York: Academic Press.

Greenberg, J. (1987). Reactions to procedural injustice in payment distributions: Do the means justify the ends? *Journal of Applied Psychology, 72*, 55–61.

Greenberg, J., & Wiethoff, C. (2001). Organizational justice as proaction and reaction: Implications for research and application. In R. Cropanzano (Ed.), *Justice in the workplace: From theory to practice* (pp. 271–302). Mahwah, NJ: Lawrence Erlbaum Associates, Inc.

Griffiths, P., & Allen, B. (1987). Assessment centres: Breaking with tradition. *Journal of Management Development, 6*(1), 18–29.

Griffiths, P., & Goodge, P. (1994). Development centres: The third generation. *Personnel Management, 26*(6), 40–46.

Hollenbeck, G. P. (1990). The past, present, and future of assessment centers. *Industrial Organizational Psychologist, 28*, 13–17.

Howard, A. (1974). An assessment of assessment centers. *Academy of Management Journal, 17*, 115–134.

Iles, P., & Forster, A. (1994). Developing organizations through collaborative developmental centers. *Organization Development Journal, 12*, 45–51.

International Task Force on Assessment Center Guidelines. (2000). Guidelines and ethical considerations for assessment center operations. *Public Personnel Management, 29*, 315–331.

Joiner, D. A. (2002). Assessment centers: What's new? *Public Personnel Management, 31*, 179–185.

Jones, R. G., & Whitmore, M. D. (1995). Evaluating developmental assessment centers as interventions: Errata. *Personnel Psychology, 48*, 562.

Klimoski, R., & Brickner, M. (1987). Why do assessment centers work? The puzzle of assessment center validity. *Personnel Psychology, 40*, 243–260.

Klimoski, R., & Strickland, W. J. (1977). Assessment centers—valid or merely prescient. *Personnel Psychology, 30*, 353–363.

Kluger, A. N., & DeNisi, A. (1996). The effects of feedback interventions on performance: A historical review, a meta-analysis, and a preliminary feedback intervention theory. *Psychological Bulletin, 119*, 254–284.

Korsgaard, M. A., & Roberson, L. (1995). Procedural justice in performance evaluation: The role of instrumental and non-instrumental voice in performance appraisal discussions. *Journal of Management, 21*, 657–669.

Kray, L. J., & Lind, E. A. (2002). The injustice of others: Social reports and the integration of others experiences in organizational justice judgments. *Organizational Behavior and Human Decision Processes, 29*, 906–924.

Lee, G. (2000). The state of the art in development centres. *Selection and Development Review, 16*(1), 10–14.

Lee, G. (2003). Same old development centres? *Selection and Development Review, 19*(5), 3–6.

Lee, G., & Beard, D. (1994). *Development centres: Realizing the potential of your employees through assessment and development.* London: McGraw-Hill.

Leventhal, G. S. (1976). Fairness in social relationships. In J. W. Thibaut, J. T. Spence, & R. C. Carson (Eds.), *Contemporary topics in social psychology* (pp. 211–240). Morristown, NJ: General Learning Press.

Leventhal, G. S. (1980). What should be done with equity theory? In K. J. Gergen, M. S. Greenberg, & H. R. Willis (Eds.), *Social exchange: Advances in theory and research* (pp. 27–55). New York: Plenum.

Liao, H., & Rupp, D. E. (2005). The impact of justice climate and justice orientation on work outcomes: A cross-level multifoci framework. *Journal of Applied Psychology, 90,* 242–256.

Lind, E. A. (1995). Justice and authority relations in organizations. In R. Cropanzano & M. K. Kacmar (Eds.), *Organizational politics, justice, and support: Managing the social climate of the workplace* (pp. 83–96). Westport, CT: Quorum Books.

Lind, E. A., Kanfer, R., Earley, P. C. (1990). Voice, control, and procedural justice: Instrumental and noninstrumental concerns in fairness judgments. *Journal of Personality and Social Psychology, 59,* 952–959.

Lind, E. A., Kray, L., & Thompson, L. (1998). The social construction of injustice: Fairness judgments in response to own and others' unfair treatment by authorities. *Organizational Behavior and Human Decision Processes, 75,* 1–22.

Lind, E. A., & Tyler, T. R. (1988). *The social psychology of procedural justice.* New York: Plenum.

Locke, E. A., & Latham, G. P. (2002). Building a practically useful theory of goal setting and task motivation: A 35-year odyssey. *American Psychologist, 57,* 705–717.

McFarlin, D. B., & Sweeney, P. D. (1996). Does having a say matter only if you get your way? Instrumental and value-expressive effects of employee voice. *Basic and Applied Social Psychology, 18,* 289–303.

Mehta, P. (1978). Dynamics of adult learning and development. *Convergence, 11,* 36–43.

Povah, N. (1986). Using assessment centers as a means for self-development. *Industrial and Commercial Training, 18,* 22–25.

Rupp, D. E., Bashshur, M. R., & Liao, H. (in press). Multilevel research in organizational justice: Theoretically-based strategies for defining and measuring justice climate. In F. J. Dansereau & F. Yammarino (Eds.), *Research in multi-level issues.* Oxford, England: Elsevier.

Rupp, D. E., & Cropanzano, R. (2002). Multifoci justice and social exchange relationships. *Organizational Behavior and Human Decision Processes, 89,* 925–946.

Salas, E., & Cannon-Bowers, J. A. (2001). The science of training: A decade of progress. *Annual Review of Psychology, 52,* 471–499.

Schleicher, D. J., Day, D. V., Mayes, B. T., & Riggio, R. E. (2002). A new frame for frame-of-reference training: Enhancing the construct validity of assessment centers. *Journal of Applied Psychology, 87,* 735–746.

Schmitt, N., Ford, J. K., & Stults, D. M. (1986). Changes in self-perceived ability as a function of performance in an assessment centre. *Journal of Occupational Psychology, 59,* 327–335.

Skarlicki, D. P., & Latham, G. P. (1996). Increasing citizenship behavior within a labor union: A test of organizational justice theory. *Journal of Applied Psychology, 81,* 161–169.

Skarlicki, D. P., & Latham, G. P. (1997). Leadership training in organizational justice to increase citizenship behavior within a labor union: A replication. *Personnel Psychology, 50,* 617–633.

Smith, P. C., & Kendall, L. M. (1963). Retranslation of expectations: An approach to the construction of unambiguous anchors for rating scales. *Journal of Applied Psychology, 47,* 149–155.

Smith-Jentsch, K. A., Salas, E., & Baker, D. P. (1996). Training team performance-related assertiveness. *Personnel Psychology, 49,* 110–116.

Spychalski, A. C., Quiñones, M. A., Gaugler, B. B., & Pohley, K. (1997). A survey of assessment center practices in organizations in the United States. *Personnel Psychology, 50,* 71–90.

Thibaut, J., & Walker, L. (1975). *Procedural justice: A psychological analysis.* Hillsdale, NJ: Lawrence Erlbaum Associates, Inc.

Thornton, G. C., III, & Cleveland, J. C. (1990). Developing managerial talent through simulation. *American Psychologist, 45,* 190–199.

Thornton, G. C., III, & Mueller-Hanson, R. A. (2004). *Developing organizational simulations: A guide for practitioners and students.* Mahwah, NJ: Lawrence Erlbaum Associates, Inc.

Thornton, G. C., III, & Rupp, D. E. (2003). Simulations and assessment centers. In J. C. Thomas (Ed.) & M. Hersen (Series Ed.), *Comprehensive handbook of psychological assessment: Vol. 4. Industrial and organizational assessment* (pp. 318–344). New York: Wiley.

Thornton, G. C., III, & Rupp, D. E. (2005). *Assessment centers in human resource management.* Mahwah, NJ: Lawrence Erlbaum Associates, Inc.

Tyler, T. R. (1997). The psychology of legitimacy: A relational perspective on voluntary deference to authorities. *Personality and Social Psychology Review, 1,* 323–345.

Tyler, T. R., Degoey, P., & Smith, H. (1996). Understanding why the justice of group procedures matters: A test of the psychological dynamics of the group-value model. *Journal of Personality and Social Psychology, 70,* 913–930.

Tyler, T., & Lind, E. A. (1992). A relational model of authority in groups. *Advances in Experimental Social Psychology, 25,* 115–191.

Tyler, T. R., Rasinski, K. A., & Spodick, N. (1985). Influence of voice on satisfaction with leaders: Exploring the meaning of process control. *Journal of Personality and Social Psychology, 48,* 72–81.

Tyler, T. R., & Smith, H. J. (1998). Social justice and social movements. In D. Gilbert, S. T. Fiske, & G. Lindzey (Eds.), *Handbook of social psychology* (Vol. 4, pp. 595–629). Boston: McGraw-Hill.

van den Bos, K., & van Prooijen, J. (2001). Referent cognitions theory: The role of closeness of reference points in the psychology of voice. *Journal of Personality and Social Psychology, 81,* 616–626.

Whitener, E. M., Brodt, S. E., Korsgaard, M. A., & Werner, J. M. (1998). Managers as initiators of trust: An exchange relationship framework for understanding managerial trustworthy behavior. *Academy of Management Review, 23,* 513–530.

THE PSYCHOLOGIST-MANAGER JOURNAL, 2006, 9(2), 171–200
Copyright © 2006 by the Society of Psychologists in Management

An Initial Validation of Developmental Assessment Centers as Accurate Assessments and Effective Training Interventions

Deborah E. Rupp, Alyssa Mitchell Gibbons,
and Amanda M. Baldwin
Department of Psychology
University of Illinois at Urbana-Champaign

Lori Anderson Snyder
Department of Psychology
University of Oklahoma

Seth M. Spain, Sang Eun Woo, Bradley J. Brummel,
and Carra S. Sims
Department of Psychology
University of Illinois at Urbana-Champaign

Myungjoon Kim
Korean Psychological Testing Institute

This article takes a critical look at the various forms of validity evidence that can be marshaled to support the effectiveness of a developmental assessment center (DAC) program. Using the holistic view of validity (American Educational Research Association, American Psychological Association, & American Council on Measurement in Education, 1999; Binning & Barrett, 1989; Messick, 1998; Society for Industrial and Organizational Psychology, 2003) as well as Kirkpatrick's (1976) taxonomy of training outcomes, we discuss how DACs can be validated in terms of both their as-

---

Correspondence should be sent to Deborah E. Rupp, Department of Psychology and Institute of Labor and Industrial Relations, University of Illinois at Urbana–Champaign, 603 East Daniel Street, Champaign, IL 61820. E-mail: derupp@uiuc.edu

sessment accuracy and their effectiveness as training interventions. Types of evidence include appropriate content; internal structure; relationships with other variables; social consequences; and reactions, learning, behavioral, and results criteria. Evidence from many of these categories is then provided from two operational DACs. Results indicate that whereas DACs may be useful tools for developing managerial competencies, continued research on this topic is needed.

Assessment centers (ACs) have long been popular as an effective strategy for selecting or promoting employees (e.g., Bray & Grant, 1966; Gaugler, Rosenthal, Thornton, & Bentson, 1987; Howard, 1997; Thornton & Byham, 1982; Thornton & Rupp, 2005). More recently, organizations have sought to use the rich information that ACs provide as a means of fostering employee development (Spychalski, Quiñones, Gaugler, & Pohley, 1997). A developmental purpose is often grafted on to an existing AC, and participants are provided with feedback about their performance in a program designed to make selection or promotion decisions (Tillema, 1998). However, organizations are increasingly creating developmental assessment centers (DACs) with the sole purpose of catalyzing development behavior (e.g., Ballantyne & Povah, 2004; Lee & Beard, 1994; Thornton & Rogers, 2001). Such centers focus on the diagnosis of current strengths and weaknesses rather than on an overall assessment of potential; they provide detailed, rather than pass–fail, behavioral feedback; and they often incorporate coaching or development planning (e.g., Ballantyne & Povah, 2004; Griffiths & Goodge, 1994). Thornton and Rupp (2005) presented an example of a possible DAC process that includes all of these elements (see Figure 1 of Rupp, Snyder, Gibbons, & Thornton, this issue, p. 75).

Though DACs are growing in popularity, much of the literature thus far has been descriptive (e.g., Cochran, Hinckle, & Dusenberry, 1987; Griffiths & Goodge, 1994; Lee & Beard, 1994) or prescriptive (e.g., Hunter, 1990; Thornton & Rogers, 2001). Very few evaluative studies of the validity of DACs have been conducted (for exceptions, see Engelbrecht & Fischer, 1995; Jones & Whitmore, 1995). Carrick and Williams (1999) commented that "the popularity of [DACs] seems to stem, at least in part, from the demonstrated criterion-related validity of the AC method" (p. 77) rather than from evidence regarding the effectiveness of DACs themselves. Although well designed, well-implemented ACs are generally useful for predicting future performance (e.g., Arthur, Day, McNelly, & Edens, 2003; Gaugler et al., 1987; Howard, 1997; Schmidt & Hunter, 1998), DACs are by their very nature interventions—the act of providing participants with feedback on their performance is intended to influence them to improve (cf. Kluger & DeNisi, 1996). The appropriate test of DAC validity, then, is not prediction but change. A valid DAC is one that provides accurate information about the dimensions measured and that results in improved performance on those dimensions (Thornton & Rupp, 2005). This dichotomy suggests that DAC programs need to be validated in two ways: as assessments and as training interventions. If the assessment is not accurate, then the feedback provided is likely to be of little use in participants' development, and accurate feedback alone is of little use if it does not lead to change.

Given the substantial differences between ACs and DACs in purpose, emphasis, and implementation, it is not clear that the established pattern of validity evidence for one will necessarily hold for the other (Carrick & Williams, 1999; Thornton & Rogers, 2001; Thornton & Rupp, 2005). In addition, although many of the means traditionally used to establish AC validity can be translated to DACs, the developmental purpose of DACs implies that a number of other types of evidence should be considered. In other words, a valid DAC should be both an accurate assessment ("valid" in the traditional testing sense of measuring what it purports to measure) and an effective training intervention (developing what it purports to develop). The present article discusses ways in which evidence can be marshaled for the validity of a DAC in both senses. For the sake of clarity, we use the term *validity* to refer to this overall validity (encompassing accuracy and effectiveness), and we use *accuracy of assessment* to refer to traditional assessment validity. The holistic view of validity (American Educational Research Association et al., 1999; Binning & Barrett, 1989; Messick, 1998; Society for Industrial and Organizational Psychology, 2003) is used as a framework for establishing accuracy and appropriateness, and Kirkpatrick's (1976) taxonomy of training outcomes is used as a framework for evaluating the effectiveness of the DAC as an intervention. To illustrate these points, we present validity evidence from two similar DACs intended for general midlevel managers.

EVIDENCE FOR DACS AS ACCURATE ASSESSMENTS

The accuracy of an assessment is a complex issue requiring many types of evidence—for example, appropriate content, internal structure, relationships with other variables, criterion relationships, and consequential validity (American Educational Research Association et al., 1999; Binning & Barrett, 1989; Messick, 1998). Many researchers have explored these types of evidence for traditional ACs and have identified a number of creative strategies for doing so (e.g., Arthur et al., 2003; Gaugler et al., 1987; Haaland & Christiansen, 2002; Lance, Lambert, Gewin, Lievens, & Conway, 2004; Lievens, 2001; Sackett, 1982). Many of these strategies, such as examining the internal structure of assessor ratings or exploring convergent and discriminant relationships between the AC dimensions and external variables, can easily be applied to the analysis of DACs. In other areas, however, such as appropriate content, DACs present additional issues that must be considered. In the following sections, we discuss ways in which the various types of accuracy and appropriateness evidence can be accumulated for DACs.

Appropriate Content

The content of an AC encompasses the behavioral dimensions being assessed, the situations simulated in the exercises, and the feedback and other information provided to participants (Thornton & Rupp, 2005). Though the issue of exercise choice and design is receiving increasing research attention (Haaland & Christiansen, 2002), the selection of content for traditional ACs is often governed by established principles and procedures (International Task Force on Assessment Center Guidelines, 2000; Thornton & Rupp, 2005). One of the most common principles in AC design is that the choice of dimensions should be based on job analysis (International Task Force on Assessment Center Guidelines, 2000) to ensure that the AC captures behavior that is relevant to job performance. Job relevance is, of course, a critical criterion in the selection of DAC dimensions; that is, there is little point in developing skills that will not be used.

For DACs, it is advisable to consider the degree to which the dimensions can realistically be developed so as to avoid creating false expectations or wasting time and effort by focusing on characteristics that are difficult to change (Carrick & Williams, 1999; Rupp, Snyder, et al., this issue, p. 75). At a minimum, it is desirable to know the time frame and the degree of difficulty that should be expected in developing a particular skill or dimension, because not all types of behavior are likely to change at the same rate (cf. Brush & Licata, 1983; Hellervik, Hazucha, & Schneider, 1992; Waters, 1980). An additional consideration is the degree to which participants perceive the dimensions as being developable. Research suggests that implicit theories about the changeability of various attributes affect individuals' development behavior with respect to those attributes (e.g., Dunning, 1995; Dweck & Leggett, 1988; Zuckerman, Gagne, & Nafshi, 2001). Taken together, these findings suggest that evidence for appropriate content in a DAC can be marshaled in three ways: one, through job analysis, showing job relevance; second, through connections with the existing training and development research literature, showing that the dimensions can be developed in at least some context; and, third, through assessing participants' beliefs about the developability of the dimensions.[1] Because DACs are often targeted at groups of "similar, but not identical" jobs (Carrick & Williams, 1999, p. 82), it may be advisable to confirm with participants that the dimensions and exercises selected are relevant to their particular positions.

Internal Structure

A common finding in the AC literature is that ratings of different dimensions within an exercise are more highly correlated than are the ratings of the same di-

---

[1]It is theoretically possible to overcome individuals' beliefs about the stability of dimensions—for example, by discussing evidence for developability at the beginning of the DAC program. However, if a large number of participants widely perceive a dimension as being unchangeable, their beliefs may represent a substantial challenge to the eventual effectiveness of the DAC.

mension across different exercises and that factor analyses of ratings of performance for each dimension made following each exercise generally cluster into exercise factors, not into dimension factors. This has led many to conclude that within-exercise dimension ratings measure only a general impression of overall performance in that exercise (e.g., Lance et al., 2004; Sackett & Tuzinski, 2001). In such a case, feedback based on dimensions would be invalid because the dimensions would not have been assessed. In traditional ACs, personnel decisions are generally based on an overall assessment rating or an aggregate of the dimension ratings, and so the lack of distinction between dimensions does not hinder prediction of performance (Howard, 1997). In DACs, however, the dimension ratings are the focus of the feedback given to the participant, on which basis he or she is expected to change his or her behavior. It is therefore of critical importance for DACs to make meaningful distinctions between dimensions (or to choose an alternate basis for giving feedback, such as task or exercise performance, though it is unclear whether this is helpful for general development; Carrick & Williams, 1999). AC scholars disagree about whether evidence for the construct validity of dimensions should be based on the dimension ratings made after each exercise or on the consensus dimension ratings made at the end of the program (cf. Howard, 1997; Lance et al., 2004). Research has more recently focused on within-exercise factors and processes as a means of understanding the ratings. For example, Lievens (2002) used standardized videotapes of assessees (for which true performance could be known) to test assessor accuracy under varying conditions, and Lievens, Chasteen, Day, and Christiansen (2004) used trait activation theory to predict which dimensions could be best assessed within a given exercise. These and other approaches to examining the rating process within individual exercises show considerable promise for illuminating this longstanding debate and clarifying the meaning of assessor ratings. Within-exercise approaches to the question of accuracy are especially relevant for DACs, because feedback is often provided for only a few exercises at a time (Ballantyne & Povah, 2004; Thornton & Rupp, 2005).

Relationships With Other Variables

Another way to evaluate the accuracy of dimension ratings is to examine their place in the nomological net—the pattern of relationships that they display with other variables that are logically related and logically independent (e.g., Cronbach, 1989). This can be done in several ways: by relating assessor dimension ratings to other measures of the same construct (e.g., a standardized situational judgment test to assess conflict management or leadership skills); by comparing dimension ratings with other types of variables, such as personality traits; or by examining the relationships among dimensions within the DAC. This last approach was taken by Shore, Thornton, and Shore (1990) and Shore, Shore, and Thornton (1992), who classified dimensions into performance-style and interpersonal-style categories.

The authors found that dimension correlations within a category (i.e., dimensions that were logically related) were higher than cross-category correlations.

Social Consequences

Messick (1998) stressed the importance of considering the social consequences of any assessment: Do the results of the assessment and the purposes for which it is used benefit society in general and the persons assessed? ACs have long been regarded as being fairer to members of minority or disadvantaged groups than other traditional assessment methods (Huck & Bray, 1976; Moses & Boehm, 1975). DACs should demonstrate fairness, especially when decisions about future training opportunities will be based on the results of the DAC. Any bias in evaluating DAC participants can lead to discriminatory practices; for example, finding that assessors rate older participants more negatively than younger participants (as observed by Clapham & Fulford, 1997; Dulewicz & Fletcher, 1982) can result in inappropriate development recommendations for those participants. Demonstrating that a DAC is accurate should include evidence that assessors' ratings are not influenced by irrelevant demographic characteristics of the participants.

EVIDENCE FOR DACS AS EFFECTIVE INTERVENTIONS

Readers may note the omission of criterion-related validity from the aforementioned discussion. Criterion-related validity for ACs has typically meant prediction of future performance (e.g., Arthur et al., 2003; Bray & Grant, 1966; Gaugler et al., 1987; Howard, 1997; Thornton & Byham, 1982; Thornton & Rupp, 2005). This is an appropriate criterion for programs designed for selection or promotion purposes, but it is a much less appropriate criterion for DACs, which are intended to catalyze behavior change. If participants respond to the feedback that they receive in a DAC and alter their behavior accordingly, the relationship between their DAC performance and their future job performance will be attenuated. In this sense, DACs form a training intervention, and it is logical to analyze them as such, using established methods for evaluating performance improvement. Development, not prediction, is the true criterion of DACs.

Many models and methods have been proposed for evaluating the effectiveness of training and development interventions (e.g., Alliger & Janak, 1989; Kirkpatrick, 1976; Kraiger, Ford, & Salas, 1993; Noe & Colquitt, 2002). Kirkpatrick's framework, identifying four levels of criteria for effectiveness, remains influential in the training and development literature despite considerable criticism (e.g., Kraiger et al., 1993). Though a range of potential learning outcomes exists (e.g., Kraiger, 2002), Kirkpatrick's model has the advantage of simplicity. Because so little systematic evaluation of DAC effectiveness has occurred to date, it seems advisable to focus for the present on broad criteria and target specific outcomes with future research. Kirkpatrick's model includes four types of criteria: participant reactions to the program, learning as an immediate result of the program, behavioral change on the job (transfer of training), and results at the organizational level. Engelbrecht and Fisher (1995) looked at behavioral criteria for one DAC, but all four levels of criteria can provide useful information regarding the effectiveness of DAC programs.

Reaction Criteria

DACs are intended to catalyze development behavior and improvement, but not all participants engage in such activities (Jones & Whitmore, 1995). Positive experiences in a DAC are no guarantee of effectiveness, but they may build self-efficacy and a desire to continue development, whereas negative experiences may have precisely the opposite effect. As a result, it is necessary to evaluate and consider participants' reactions to the DAC and their perceptions of benefit from it. Participants' engagement in development activities within the program may also be an indicator of their reactions. If feedback is provided at multiple time points during the DAC (e.g., Ballantyne & Povah, 2004; Thornton & Rupp, 2005), participants may respond to and incorporate the feedback into their behavior in subsequent exercises. This assimilation indicates that they take the feedback seriously and are willing to follow the recommendations that they have been given.

Learning Criteria

If participants are engaging in active learning during the program, it may be possible to observe immediate improvement in some simple behaviors (e.g., giving a formal presentation; Waters, 1980). Recognizing such improvement may help to build participants' self-efficacy for learning (Hellervik et al., 1992; McCaulay & Hezlett, 2001) and encourage further development efforts. Although several theoretical models exist that predict differences in the time frames needed for development of different skills (Brush & Licata, 1983; Hellervik et al., 1992; Waters, 1980), there is as yet little empirical evidence to confirm these time frames. Investigating the degree to which within-program change occurs in DACs can help fill out these theoretical models and enhance understanding of the overall development process.

Behavioral Criteria

Behavioral criteria, or measures of behavioral transfer to the job setting, may be the most important learning outcomes for DACs. Even if reactions are positive and within-program change occurs, there is still little benefit if participants cannot apply their development experiences on the job. Engelbrecht and Fisher (1995) compared the performance of DAC participants and a control group of managers 3 months following the DAC program. They found significant differences between participants and controls on six of eight dimensions. Engelbrecht and Fisher used supervisors' ratings of performance on the dimensions, but multisource ratings (including self-ratings and subordinate ratings, in addition to supervisor ratings) may provide additional insight into participants' development. It is possible that different sources perceive development in different ways or at different times. Participants, for example, may perceive real changes in their own behavior that may not be readily or immediately observable to others (Hellervik et al., 1992). Using multisource ratings, however, can be problematic because the accuracy of such ratings is difficult to determine and many different motives can influence raters (e.g., Byham, 2003). An alternative approach is to measure change directly by creating a parallel, second DAC (Brummel & Spain, 2005) and reassessing participants after a substantial time interval.

Results Criteria

Although individual-level development is usually the goal of DACs, organization-level impact data are needed to justify the continuation of such programs. Reconciling individual-level and organization-level change is difficult because individuals are likely to change in different ways and at different rates in response to the same intervention (Smither, London, & Reilly, 2005). Aggregation of individual effects may represent one solution to this problem. Another approach might be to consider indirect effects of development, such as changes in subordinates' satisfaction as their supervisors develop (e.g., Atwater, Brett, & Ryan, 2004).

The current study presents preliminary findings from two operational DACs that address many of the kinds of validity evidence described here. Specifically, data related to appropriate content, internal structure, relationships among dimensions, social consequences, participant reactions, within-program change (knowledge), and postprogram change (behavior) are discussed.

METHOD

Overview

Midlevel managers from several different organizations participated in one of two 1-day DACs. The DACs were identical in structure (number and type of exercises, dimensions, etc.), but the specific exercise content differed. The DACs operated over a period of 2 years; all participants in Year 1 experienced DAC 1 and all participants in Year 2 experienced DAC 2. In both, participants completed six simulation exercises and received detailed behavioral feedback about their performance relative to eight behavioral dimensions. Multisource ratings of participants' job performance were collected from participants, their supervisors, and their subordinates (when applicable), both immediately before and 1 to 4 months after participation. Both DACs were explicitly developmental; no data were used for personnel decision making, although participants received feedback and assistance in setting development goals. All feedback was provided directly to participants and not to their supervisors or human resource departments.

Participants

In all, 207 managers from 22 Midwestern organizations participated in the program ($n = 100$, DAC 1; $n = 107$, DAC 2). Twenty-two of the DAC 2 participants had previously completed DAC 1 and were returning for reassessment. These participants were counted only once for the descriptive statistics presented in this section. Participants in DAC 1 and DAC 2 did not significantly differ on demographic characteristics, with the exception of tenure in the participants' current organizations (discussed later). The combined sample was predominantly Caucasian (89%) but almost evenly divided between men (45%) and women (53%).[2] The average age of the participants was 41.0 years, with an average of 19.9 years of experience in the workforce. The industries represented by the participants included banking, manufacturing, county and city government, construction, research, and postsecondary education. In sum, 72% of the participants identified themselves as middle managers, 14% as lower-level management, and 14% as upper management.

Dimensions

Eight dimensions were assessed in the DACs: problem solving, oral communication, leadership, conflict management, information seeking, planning and organizing, fairness, and cultural adaptability (see Table 1 for dimension definitions). Five dimensions were assessed in each exercise. The same dimensions were assessed in both DACs, with dimensions mapping to the same exercises in each. Choice of the first six dimensions was based on work by Gibbons, Rupp, Snyder, Holub, and Woo (this issue, p. 99), who synthesized several influential models of managerial performance to identify dimensions that were common to most managerial jobs and suitable for inclusion in a DAC. This procedure represents a departure from the traditional method of establishing dimensions through job analysis; however, because participants represented a variety of diverse industries, organizations, and position titles, a general model of managerial performance was needed. The performance models used by Gibbons, Rupp, et al. were based on job analyses from

---

[2]Demographic information was not available for 4 participants.

TABLE 1
Dimensions and Subdimensions

Dimension	Subdimensions
Problem solving	Identifies problems, perceives logical relationships among problems or issues
	Develops courses of action to determine costs and benefits of each; evaluates the outcomes of a problem solution
	Makes timely and logical decisions
Oral communication	Speaks (both verbally and nonverbally) with clarity in message, pitch, volume, and gesture
	Conveys message that is straightforward and concise
	Matches communication style with audience
Leadership	Guides, directs, and motivates others using regular, specific, and constructive feedback
	Balances the interests, abilities, goals, and priorities of self and others with the needs of the organization
	Commands attention and respect; promotes positive change
Conflict management	Possesses an effective strategy for dealing with conflict
	Recognizes and openly addresses conflict appropriately
	Arrives at constructive solutions while maintaining positive working relationships
Information seeking	Gets information from multiple sources
	Finds all relevant information for the situation
	Organizes the information into usable patterns
Planning and organizing	Makes short- and long-term goals
	Determines priorities and allocates time and resources by recognizing time limitations
	Systematically monitors tasks and activities of self or others to ensure accomplishment of specific objectives
Fairness	Displays sensitivity to the needs, feelings, and viewpoints of others; expresses honesty, sincerity, neutrality, courtesy, respect, and dignity; provides others with the appropriate levels of choice over their situation; allows others to express their opinions
	Delivers all agreed-upon outcomes as promised
	Maintains a consistent standard of treatment for all employees; shares information; provides proper evidence/explanation of actions taken
Cultural adaptability	Refrains from premature judgments about people and seeks information to better understand cultural differences
	Makes correct attributions regarding the behavior of others
	Communicates in a culturally appropriate and appreciative manner (values others' viewpoints, ideas, opinions, judgments, beliefs, and personalities)

many jobs, industries, and organizations (e.g., Borman & Brush, 1993; Tett, Guterman, Bleier, & Murphy, 2000) and can be expected to contain dimensions relevant for most managerial positions. Fairness and cultural adaptability were included as experimental, or secondary, dimensions. Although these dimensions did not appear in most of the managerial performance taxonomies, a growing body of research indicates that treating subordinates and colleagues fairly (e.g., Colquitt, Conlon, Wesson, Porter, & Ng, 2001; Johnston, 1991) and interacting with members of different cultures (e.g., Bhawuk, 2001; Landis & Bhagat, 1996) are important skills for modern managers.

Exercises and Program Structure

Each DAC consisted of six simulation exercises arranged into two parallel blocks of three exercises each, following Thornton and Rupp's DAC process model (2005) presented in Figure 1 of Rupp, Snyder, et al. (this issue, p. 75). Each block consisted of a leaderless group discussion, a case study with oral presentation, and an interview simulation. Participants completed the first block of exercises in the morning and then received feedback from an assessor. The feedback was narrative in form and organized around the dimensions. In the afternoon, participants completed the second block of exercises and again received feedback. After each block, participants were provided with self-reflection forms on which they could evaluate their performance on the dimensions before meeting with the assessor. At the conclusion of the program, participants submitted anonymous program evaluation forms in which they were asked to indicate their reactions to and perceptions of several aspects of the program—including the exercises, dimensions, feedback, and program staff—using 7-point Likert scales, with scores of 1 indicating very negative reactions and scores of 7 indicating very positive ones.

Each participant was observed by three assessors in the course of the day. Assessors used behaviorally anchored rating scales to evaluate participants. On the scales, each dimension was divided into three subdimensions, and assessors noted relevant behavioral observations and provided ratings for each. Table 1 shows the subdimensions for each dimension. Each subdimension was rated on a 7-point Likert scale, with a score of 4 representing adequate performance, a score of 1 indicating very poor performance, and a score of 7 indicating exceptional performance. Assessors discussed their behavioral observations in an integration session to arrive at consensus feedback for each participant on each dimension. Assessors had access to all assessors' ratings and observations during this session.

Assessors

Assessors were graduate students in human resource management or industrial–organizational psychology and local certified human resource professionals working in the field. Assessors completed a 4-day certification program that included going through the DAC as a participant, training on how to avoid observation and rating errors (Hedge & Kavanagh, 1988; Pulakos, 1984), establishing a common frame of reference regarding performance on each dimension and subdimension (Schleicher, Day, Mayes, & Riggio, 2002), and learning techniques for giving feedback.

Multisource Ratings

Self-ratings and supervisor and subordinate ratings of the participants' performance on the dimensions were collected before participation and again 1 to 4 months following the DAC. Participants and their raters in DAC 1 were sent paper surveys, with a cover letter explaining the purpose of the survey and how their responses would be used. They were asked to return the surveys either directly to the researchers or through a designated contact person within their organization (in signed, sealed envelopes) at their discretion. In DAC 2, the survey was the same, but raters with Internet access were contacted via e-mail and provided with an access code and a link to an online version of the survey. The consent letter was included in the e-mail message. Raters for DAC 2 participants who did not have Internet access followed the same paper-survey procedure used in DAC 1. All sources rated the participant on each of the 24 subdimensions (i.e., a three-item measure for each dimension) using a 7-point Likert scale from 1 (*needs improvement*) to 7 (*highly proficient*). Organizations were asked to encourage rater participation via a memo or e-mail from the organizational contact person. All raters were informed that their participation was voluntary and confidential and that they would help the ratee to develop his or her skills as a manager.

RESULTS

Accuracy of Assessment

Appropriate content.   As discussed, dimensions for the DACs were based on an extensive review of the managerial performance literature. Consequently, these dimensions were expected to be applicable to the majority of midlevel managers. To verify that this was indeed the case for this specific group of participants, several items regarding the content of the program were included in the anonymous program evaluation. Answers to these items were evaluated in two ways: one, by counting the number of participants who gave positive responses (5, 6, or 7) and, two, by conducting one-sample t tests to investigate whether the mean score represented a significant deviation from the neutral point (4). Of all the participants, 96% of DAC 1 and 79% of DAC 2 agreed with the statement "the competencies [dimensions] are relevant to my job," and 71% of DAC 1 and 67% of DAC 2 indicated that the situations represented in the exercises were appropriate for their jobs. Nearly all participants—93% of DAC 1 and 89% of DAC 2—found the role-players in the interview simulations believable. For the dimension, exercise, and role-player items, the means were significantly greater than 4, indicating that participants generally endorsed the items positively: DAC 1, dimensions, $t(4) = 14.42, p < .01$, exercises, $t(44) = 5.25, p < .01$, role-players, $t(44) = 13.50, p < .01$; DAC 2, dimensions, $t(86) = 10.81, p < .01$, exercises, $t(87) = 5.86, p < .01$, role-players, $t(87) = 15.37, p < .01$. To investigate whether participants perceived the exercises as being at an appropriate level of difficulty, the evaluation contained two items: "the exercises were too difficult" and "the exercises were too easy." Mean scores on both items were both significantly below the neutral point, indicating that respondents disagreed: DAC 1, too difficult, $t(44) = -4.49, p < .01$, too easy, $t(44) = -6.44, p < .01$; DAC 2, too difficult, $t(88) = -5.45, p < .01$, too easy, $t(87) = -8.56, p < .01$. In sum, 89% of DAC 1 and 74% of DAC 2 participants gave negative or neutral responses (4 or less) to both items, indicating that the exercises were neither too hard nor too easy but rather "just right."

Internal structure.   A unique feature of the present study was that the rating scales used by assessors divided each dimension into three subdimensions (Table 1). This permitted us to conduct within-exercise confirmatory factor analyses to explore whether assessor ratings within each exercise differentiated between dimensions or reflected general halo error. If the ratings made within a single exercise are described by a single-factor model, it is likely that halo was present, but a multifactor model implies that differentiation between dimensions occurred. A single-factor and a five-factor model were tested for each of the 6 exercises in each DAC (12 exercises total). In all cases, the five-factor model showed significantly better fit than the single-factor model, suggesting that assessor ratings reflected more than a general exercise or halo factor (see Tables 2 and 3 for fit comparisons). Fit indexes for the five-factor models approach, but do not attain, the usual criteria for goodness of fit (e.g., root mean squared error of approximation < .05, Normed Fit Index > .90; Bentler & Bonett, Tucker–Lewis Index > .90; Tucker & Lewis, 1973) for most exercises. However, the afternoon group discussion in DAC 1, the afternoon group discussion in DAC 2, and the morning and afternoon interview simulations in DAC 2 all appear to show reasonably good fit.

Relationships with other variables.   Dimensions were classified into performance-style and interpersonal-style clusters. Based on the classification system of Shore and colleagues (1990), information seeking, planning and organizing, problem solving, and oral communication were considered performance-style dimensions; and leadership, conflict management, fairness,[3] and cultural adaptability were considered interpersonal-style dimensions. Because dimension ratings

---

[3]Fairness and cultural adaptability were each assessed in only one block in each DAC.

TABLE 2

Comparison of Fit for Single-Factor and Five-Factor Models —
Developmental Assessment Center (DAC) 1

Exercise	Fit Indices	Single-Factor Model	Five-Factor Model	Fit Comparison
Group discussion 1	χ^2	158.94	120.31	$\Delta \chi^2 = 38.63$
	df	90.00	80.00	$\Delta df = 10$
	χ^2/df	1.77	1.50	$p < .01$
	RMSEA	0.10	0.08	
	NFI	0.83	0.87	
	TLI	0.91	0.94	
Interview simulation 1	χ^2	197.64	163.27	$\Delta \chi^2 = 34.37$
	df	90.00	80.00	$\Delta df = 10$
	χ^2/df	2.20	2.04	$p < .01$
	RMSEA	0.12	0.11	
	NFI	0.77	0.81	
	TLI	0.84	0.86	
Case study/presentation 1	χ^2	210.78	139.48	$\Delta \chi^2 = 71.30$
	df	90.00	80.00	$\Delta df = 10$
	χ^2/df	2.34	1.74	$p < .01$
	RMSEA	0.12	0.09	
	NFI	0.78	0.85	
	TLI	0.83	0.91	
Group discussion 2	χ^2	189.39	118.29	$\Delta \chi^2 = 71.10$
	df	90.00	80.00	$\Delta df = 10$
	χ^2/df	2.10	1.48	$p < .01$
	RMSEA	0.11	0.08	
	NFI	0.84	0.90	
	TLI	0.90	0.95	
Interview simulation 2	χ^2	331.49	178.91	$\Delta \chi^2 = 152.58$
	df	90.00	80.00	$\Delta df = 10$
	χ^2/df	3.68	2.24	$p < .01$
	RMSEA	0.17	0.12	
	NFI	0.69	0.83	
	TLI	0.71	0.87	
Case study/presentation 2	χ^2	319.43	167.29	$\Delta \chi^2 = 152.14$
	df	90.00	80.00	$\Delta df = 10$
	χ^2/df	3.55	2.09	$p < .01$
	RMSEA	0.18	0.12	
	NFI	0.66	0.82	
	TLI	0.68	0.86	

Note. df = degrees of freedom; RMSEA = root mean squared error of approximation; NFI = normed fit index (Bentler & Bonett, 1980); TLI = Tucker Lewis index (Tucker & Lewis, 1973).

TABLE 3

Comparison of Fit for Single-Factor and Five-Factor Models —
Developmental Assessment Center (DAC) 2

Exercise	Fit Indices	Single-Factor Model	Five-Factor Model	Fit Comparison
Group discussion 3	χ^2	197.38	171.53	$\Delta\chi^2 = 25.85$
	df	90.00	80.00	$\Delta df = 10$
	χ^2/df	2.19	2.14	$p < .01$
	RMSEA	0.13	0.13	
	NFI	0.79	0.89	
	TLI	0.85	0.86	
Interview simulation 3	χ^2	200.05	109.28	$\Delta\chi^2 = 90.77$
	df	90.00	80.00	$\Delta df = 10$
	X^2/df	2.22	1.37	$p < .01$
	RMSEA	0.11	0.06	
	NFI	0.84	0.91	
	TLI	0.89	0.97	
Case study/presentation 3	χ^2	216.07	115.61	$\Delta\chi^2 = 100.46$
	df	90.00	80.00	$\Delta df = 10$
	χ^2/df	2.40	1.45	$p < .01$
	RMSEA	0.12	0.07	
	NFI	0.77	0.88	
	TLI	0.83	0.94	
Group discussion 4	χ^2	196.64	109.62	$\Delta\chi^2 = 87.02$
	df	90.00	80.00	$\Delta df = 10$
	χ^2/df	2.18	1.37	$p < .01$
	RMSEA	0.11	0.06	
	NFI	0.81	0.90	
	TLI	0.87	0.96	
Interview simulation 4	χ^2	232.57	115.81	$\Delta\chi^2 = 116.77$
	df	90.00	80.00	$\Delta df = 10$
	χ^2/df	2.58	1.45	$p < .01$
	RMSEA	0.13	0.07	
	NFI	0.82	0.91	
	TLI	0.86	0.96	
Case study/presentation 4	χ^2	267.32	136.77	$\Delta\chi^2 = 130.55$
	df	90.00	80.00	$\Delta df = 10$
	χ^2/df	2.97	1.71	$p < .01$
	RMSEA	0.14	0.09	
	NFI	0.76	0.87	
	TLI	0.79	0.92	

Note. df = degrees of freedom; RMSEA = root mean squared error of approximation; NFI = normed fit index (Bentler & Bonett, 1980); TLI = Tucker Lewis index (Tucker & Lewis, 1973).

TABLE 4
Average Correlations Between Performance-Style and
Interpersonal-Style Dimensions

	DAC 1 Block 1	DAC 1 Block 2	DAC 2 Block 1	DAC 2 Block 2
Performance-style dimensions	.60	.63	.63	.64
Interpersonal-style dimensions	.70	.67	.77	.77
Performance-style × Interpersonal-style dimensions	.61	.58	.62	.59

Note. Performance-style dimensions are information seeking, planning and organizing, problem solving, and oral communication. Interpersonal-style dimensions are leadership, conflict management, fairness (Block 1 only) and cultural adaptability (Block 2 only). DAC = developmental assessment center.

were aggregated at the block level, each exercise block was analyzed separately, for a total of four blocks: morning and afternoon blocks in both DAC 1 and DAC 2. Table 4 shows the average correlations among performance-style dimensions, among interpersonal-style dimensions, and between dimensions in different clusters. Overall, the average correlation among interpersonal-style dimensions was higher (average $r = .73$) than the that between dimensions in different clusters (average $r = .60$), but the performance-style dimensions had only slightly higher correlations (average $r = .62$).[4] These results provide only slight support for the classifications suggested by Shore and colleagues.

Social consequences.   No consistent age or gender biases were found in either DAC. There was a significant positive correlation, $r = .21$, $p < .05$, between age and leadership in the first block of DAC 1; however, it is possible that this effect reflects differences in experience (which are relevant to performance) rather than an age bias or distortion. In DAC 1 there were no significant effects of gender, but in DAC 2 women received significantly lower ratings than did men on leadership in the first block, $t(91) = 2.15$, $p < .05$, and on problem solving in the second block, $t(91) = 2.14$, $p < .05$. However, scores on the same dimension in the other block (i.e., leadership in the second block and problem solving in the first) were similar for both genders, and there were no differences on other dimensions. This does not suggest a strong or pervasive bias, consistent with findings from traditional ACs that suggest that ACs are fair to members of minority or disadvantaged groups (e.g., Huck & Bray, 1976; Moses & Boehm, 1975). Because 89% of the overall sample came from Caucasian backgrounds, effects of ethnicity were not tested.

---

[4]If oral communication is considered an interpersonal-style dimension instead of a performance-style dimension, the average correlation for interpersonal-style dimensions reduces to $r = .65$ and the other correlations remain the same.

EFFECTIVENESS OF INTERVENTION

Reaction Criteria

Participant reactions, as expressed in the anonymous program evaluations, were generally positive, though there were differences between the two DACs. Participants appeared to consider the feedback valid: 100% of DAC 1 and 91% of DAC 2 participants agreed with the statement "the feedback I received seemed accurate." Additionally, 96% of DAC 1 and 88% of DAC 2 participants agreed that the feedback was helpful. Participants also reported engaging in development-related behavior during the DACs. In sum, 98% of DAC 1 and 87% of DAC 2 participants indicated that they had identified at least one developmental need, and 89% of DAC 1 and 71% of DAC 2 participants agreed that they were more aware of their developmental needs as a result of attending the program. Furthermore, 95% of DAC 1 and 81% of DAC 2 noted that they had tried at least one new approach or behavior in the exercises, indicating engagement in active learning and exploration. Finally, 100% of DAC 1 and 70% of DAC 2 participants noted that they had set at least one development goal for future improvement.[5]

Learning Criteria

To assess within-program change, multivariate analyses of variance (MANOVAs) were conducted in which the exercise block (morning or afternoon) was treated as a repeated-measures independent variable and assessor ratings on each dimension were treated as the dependent variables. Because fairness was assessed in the morning and cultural adaptability in the afternoon, within-program change was not estimated for these dimensions. Separate analyses were conducted for DAC 1 and DAC 2. In the DAC 1 analysis, there was a significant multivariate effect, $F(6, 91)$ = 4.97, $p < .01$, but the only significant univariate effect was for oral communication, $F(1, 96) = 14.32, p < .01$. For DAC 2, the multivariate effect was again significant, $F(6, 101) = 13.02, p < .01$, and significant univariate effects appeared for oral communication, $F(1, 106) = 13.67, p < .01$, planning and organizing, $F(1, 106) = 14.10, p < .01$, leadership, $F(1, 106) = 23.78, p < .01$, and problem solving, $F(1, 106) = 11.41, p < .01$. For all significant effects, mean-level changes were positive, except for problem solving in DAC 2, which decreased from morning to afternoon (see Table 5 for dimension means). A possible explanation for this is that the after-

---

[5]The discrepancy between the DACs is largest for this item, but the reason is most likely a procedural change instituted for DAC 2. In DAC 1, short-term goal setting was an explicit component of the afternoon feedback session, but participants and assessors reported that time constraints and limited resources made it difficult to set useful goals, and many of the goals produced were of low quality. In DAC 2, the final feedback session encouraged participants to consider possible goals, but goals were not officially set until a phone meeting with the assessor approximately 1 month after participation.

noon exercises generally focused on more ambiguous problems than did the morning exercises. For example, in DAC 1 the morning group-discussion exercise asked participants to decide whether to terminate or retain several "problem" employees (a structured task), whereas the afternoon group-discussion exercise involved generating recommendations to facilitate a merger (a much less structured task).

Participants' own perceptions of their performance generally concurred with the assessors' evaluations. Participants were asked to rate their performance on each dimension as part of the self-reflection activity following each block. The MANOVA analyses described earlier were repeated, treating participants' self-ratings as the dependent variables, instead of the assessor ratings. Again, for DAC 1 there was a significant multivariate effect, $F(6, 89) = 2.52, p < .05$, and a significant univariate effect for oral communication, $F(1, 94) = 9.53, p < .01$. For DAC 2, there was a significant multivariate effect, $F(6, 79) = 21.55, p < .01$, and univariate effects were significant for all six dimensions. All significant mean-level changes were positive (see Table 5). The afternoon self-evaluation form included items that asked participants directly if they had perceived changes in their performance on each dimension. They were asked to compare their morning and afternoon performances on a 7-point scale ranging from 1 (*better in the morning*) to 7 (*better in the afternoon*). The neutral point (4) was labeled *about the same*. A series of one-sample t tests was conducted to determine whether participants' responses were significantly different from the neutral point. In DAC 1, this was the case for information seeking, $t(94) = 3.13, p < .01$, leadership, $t(94) = 2.30, p < .05$, and oral communication, $t(94) = 1.99, p < .05$. In DAC 2, participants reported better afternoon performances for all six dimensions: information seeking, $t(94) = 6.70, p < .01$, leadership, $t(92) = 7.23, p < .01$, oral communication, $t(92) = 6.78, p < .01$, planning and organizing, $t(93) = 6.31, p < .01$, problem solving, $t(92) = 7.42, p < .01$, and conflict management, $t(93) = 8.12, p < .01$.

Behavioral Criteria

For DAC 1, pre- and post-DAC self-ratings were available for 28 participants; subordinate ratings were available for 43; and supervisor ratings were available for 9. As a result, supervisor ratings were not considered in the following analysis for DAC 1. For DAC 2, pre- and post-DAC self-ratings were available for 29 participants, subordinate ratings for 39, and supervisor ratings for 28. MANOVAs were conducted treating time (preparticipation or postparticipation) as a repeated-measures independent variable and the source's ratings on the dimensions as the dependent variables. Because not all sources were available for all participants, self-ratings and subordinate ratings were analyzed separately. For participants with more than one subordinate, subordinate ratings were averaged before conducting the MANOVA so as to yield one score per dimension per participant.

TABLE 5
Within-Program Change in Dimension Ratings

		Info Seek	Plan Org	Prob Solv	Oral Comm	Leadership	Conf Mgmt
DAC 1							
Assessor ratings	Block 1	4.83	4.50	4.67	4.66*	4.73	4.92
	Block 2	4.77	4.44	4.52	4.97*	4.67	4.74
Self ratings	Block 1	4.67	4.61	4.42	4.18*	4.45	4.55
	Block 2	4.77	4.61	4.56	4.66*	4.68	4.45
DAC 2							
Assessor ratings	Block 1	4.42	4.07*	4.41*	4.39*	3.94*	4.01
	Block 2	4.46	4.35*	4.17*	4.63*	4.37*	4.19
Self ratings	Block 1	4.43*	4.36*	4.47*	4.22*	4.18*	4.02*
	Block 2	5.20*	5.18*	5.20*	5.14*	5.27*	5.19*

Note. DAC = developmental assessment center; Info Seek = information seeking; Plan Org = planning and organizing; Prob Solv = problem solving; Oral Comm = oral communication; Conf Mgmt = conflict management.

*The difference between blocks meets statistical significance criteria, $p < .05$.

For DAC 1, the MANOVA for self-ratings showed a significant main effect of time, $F(8, 20) = 3.11, p < .05$. Significant effects were found at the univariate level for four of the eight dimensions: conflict management, $F(1, 27) = 12.67, p < .01$, oral communication, $F(1, 27) = 4.86, p < .05$, leadership, $F(1, 27) = 5.64, p < .05$, and cultural adaptability, $F(1, 27) = 10.33, p < .01$. Mean-level changes were positive for all four dimensions, indicating that participants perceived improvement (see Table 6). Effects for other dimensions were not significant at the univariate level, but all means were in the predicted direction of positive change. The MANOVA for subordinate ratings found no significant multivariate effect, $F(8, 35) = 0.99, p > .05$. However, all mean differences were again in the predicted direction. For DAC 2, none of the MANOVAs (self-ratings or subordinate or supervisor ratings) showed a significant multivariate effect of time. The small sample size used in these analyses suggests that the results should be viewed with caution.

DISCUSSION

The collection of validity evidence for DACs is a complex process because DACs must demonstrate validity as assessment tools and training interventions. Many types of evidence are needed to establish a case for either of these criteria; demonstrating both requires a still broader body of evidence. Although establishing predictive validity is often the primary object for traditional ACs, this is in many ways the least useful type of evidence for DACs, which are intended to cause changes in future performance. The present article provides an example of how established frameworks for validating assessments and development programs can be integrated to investigate the validity of DACs.

Validity as Assessments

Many of the techniques used to validate traditional ACs are equally appropriate for the validation of DACs, such as using job analysis to verify that the content is appropriate and exploring the convergent and discriminant validity of logically related dimensions. The pattern of results obtained in the present study was generally consistent with findings for traditional ACs. The dimensions chosen, though not based directly on job analysis, were perceived as being relevant by most participants. Assessors' ratings did not appear to be influenced by demographic characteristics of the participants, and participants reported that they perceived benefits from engaging in the program. These results imply that the DACs used were reasonably appropriate for the participants involved. Evidence regarding convergent and discriminant relationships among variables is less clear. Analysis of correlations between theoretically related and unrelated dimensions found only slight

TABLE 6
Comparisons of Self, Subordinate, and Supervisor Ratings on Dimensions Before and After Participation

		n^a	Info Seek	Plan Org	Prob Solv	Oral Comm	Leadership	Conf Mgmt	Fairness	Cult Adapt
DAC 1										
Self-ratings	Pre	28	5.55	5.04	5.36	4.95*	5.02*	4.73*	5.57	5.40*
	Post	28	5.65	5.23	5.65	5.32*	5.36*	5.29*	5.90	5.96*
Sub-ratings	Pre	43	5.18	4.69*	5.13	5.22	4.97	4.73	5.22	5.36
	Post	43	5.39	4.99*	5.29	5.30	5.07	4.97	5.36	5.52
DAC 2										
Self-ratings	Pre	29	5.51	4.85	5.44	4.83	4.87	4.67	5.29	5.15
	Post	29	5.62	5.03	5.37	5.13	5.09	4.84	5.33	5.28
Sub-ratings	Pre	39	5.16	4.70	5.08	4.89	4.81	4.56	5.10	5.32
	Post	39	5.31	4.98	5.13	5.12	4.92	4.71	5.18	5.32
Super-ratings	Pre	28	5.45	5.14	4.99	4.87	4.90*	4.70*	5.51	5.58
	Post	28	5.46	5.21	5.23	5.18	5.32*	5.13*	5.68	5.85

Note. DAC = developmental assessment center; Info Seek = information seeking; Plan Org = planning and organizing; Prob Solv = problem solving; Oral Comm = oral communication; Conf Mgmt = conflict management; Cult Adapt = cultural adaptability.

^{a}Only participants for whom both pre- and postparticipation ratings were available from the same source were included in these analyses.

*Univariate difference meets statistical significance criteria, $p < .05$.

support for the clusters suggested by previous research (e.g., Shore, Thornton, & Shore, 1990), and no external measures of the dimensions were available.

With respect to internal structure of assessor ratings, the overall pattern of correlations between dimension ratings across exercises was consistent with that found by many other AC researchers (e.g., Lance, Newbolt, Gatewood, Foster, French, & Smith, 2000; Lance et al., 2004; Sackett & Tuzinski, 2001). Correlations between different dimensions in the same exercise were, on average, higher than correlations between the same dimension measured in different exercises. Such findings are generally believed to indicate a lack of accuracy, in that assessors are not distinguishing between dimensions but rather making ratings based on a general impression of exercise performance at best (Lance et al., 2000) or a serious and pervasive halo error at worst (Sackett & Tuzinski, 2001). In either case, feedback regarding strengths and weaknesses on the dimensions carries little meaning because assessors have not made such distinctions during the exercises. However, the within-exercise factor analyses tell a somewhat different story. They indicate that assessors did make distinctions, to some extent, among the dimensions and that a single-factor model was not sufficient to describe assessors' ratings.

The reason for this result is not yet clear. It can be argued that it is simply a function of dividing the dimensions into subdimensions—that artificial factors were created by essentially asking assessors to make the same rating three times. Inspection of the data, however, suggests that assessors did make distinctions between subdimensions. Across both DACs, assessors gave the same rating to all three subdimensions on only 17% of the dimensions that they assessed. Another possibility is that the subdivided rating scale primed the assessors to distinguish between dimensions more than they would have under other circumstances. If the ratings that assessors are making on the dimensions correspond to true differences in dimension proficiency, such a scale may be a useful aid to assessors in organizing their observations. If, however, assessors are making arbitrary distinctions between dimensions when no true performance differences exist, feedback based on those distinctions would not be valid. Lievens (2002) found that assessors were capable of identifying real differences in dimension performance, but he suggested that such differences may seldom occur in practice. To fully test this explanation, better measures of "true" dimension performance are needed. Still another explanation is that the developmental purpose of the program may have encouraged assessors to look for differences in dimension performance because they were aware that they would be giving feedback to participants regarding their strengths and weaknesses. Research on performance appraisal ratings indicates that the purpose of the appraisal affects not only the ratings themselves but also the cognitive processes used by the raters (e.g., Zedeck & Cascio, 1982) and that ratings made for developmental purposes are sometimes more accurate than those made for administrative purposes (Murphy & Cleveland, 1995). We are not presently aware of any research that extends this work to ACs, however, so the viability of this explanation remains to be tested.

Validity as Training Interventions

Because the criterion for DACs is performance improvement, it is reasonable to establish criterion-related validity by evaluating the effectiveness of the DAC as a training intervention. Kirkpatrick's (1976) taxonomy was used as the framework for this initial validation. Participant reactions to the program were generally positive, but reactions were more positive to DAC 1 than to DAC 2. Within-program improvements indicate some slight progress with respect to knowledge criteria. Participants perceived greater performance gains than did assessors, but this is perhaps to be expected because participants are more aware of their own internal efforts to change (Hellervik et al., 1992). Behavioral criteria, assessed through multisource ratings before and after participation, indicate that participants perceived improvement on four of the eight dimensions within a few months of the program. Their subordinates, however, perceived changes for one dimension, and not enough change to create an effect at the multivariate level. However, means for all dimensions were in the predicted direction for both groups (i.e., postprogram ratings were higher than preprogram ratings). Power in the MANOVA analyses was low due to the small number of participants for whom follow-up data were available, which may have precluded finding stronger results.

Smither et al. (2005) conducted a meta-analysis of longitudinal studies of the effectiveness of multisource feedback programs. The authors calculated an uncorrected effect size of .24 on subordinate ratings and an uncorrected effect size of .00 on self-ratings. We used the formula provided by Smither and colleagues for repeated-measures designs to calculate uncorrected effect sizes for the change perceived on each dimension by DAC 1 participants and their subordinates. For self-ratings, effect sizes ranged from .12 to .60 with an average effect size of .39 across all dimensions. For subordinate ratings, the dimension effect sizes ranged from .11 to .38, with an average of .21. Though the present findings are based on a small sample and should not be overinterpreted, they suggest that the improvement observed by DAC 1 participants and their subordinates was comparable to that occurring as a result of multisource feedback interventions.[6]

Smither and colleagues (2005) also discussed a number of factors that are likely to affect the development of individual participants, and they argued that it is not reasonable to expect large across-the-board improvement for all participants, especially in a short time. They noted that individuals who receive feedback on multiple dimensions usually target their development efforts to those areas identified as growth needs or weaknesses, rather than seek to improve equally in all areas. Individual differences and organizational context factors play major roles in their model of development, which can easily be extended to apply to DACs and other types of interventions.

---

[6]Note that feedback from the multisource ratings in DAC 1 was not provided to participants until after the follow-up ratings had been collected.

The use of participants from multiple organizations precluded tests of results criteria, or the effectiveness of the DACs in improving organization-level performance. To our knowledge, no studies of this kind have been conducted. The arguments made by Smither et al. (2005) imply that the individual, not the organization, may be the most appropriate unit for assessing change. However, DACs are far from inexpensive, and more precise estimates of probable benefits are needed to justify their continuing use in organizations. Much future research is needed to establish whether, when, and how much change can be expected (for which types of dimensions or skills) as a result of participating in a DAC. In addition to such information at the individual level, a full test of results criteria would require well-measured unit-level performance criteria, clearly established links between individual performance and unit performance, and the ability to control for the many extraneous factors that may affect unit performance. Such a test might be most feasible in, for example, a manufacturing organization operating identically structured plants in multiple locations, with employees from some plants participating in a DAC and with those of the other plants serving as a control group, provided that external variables such as regional economic conditions are controlled statistically.

Study Strengths

The present study makes several unique contributions to the study of DACs and their usefulness for improving performance. It illustrates the many ways in which validity evidence for DACs can be accumulated, and it connects the question of DAC validity to frameworks for validating assessments and training interventions. It also provides examples of many types of evidence for two similar DACs, much of which is positive. This evidence is based on a broad sample of managers from a variety of different industries, organizations, and position titles. This study took an innovative approach to the question of the internal structure of assessor ratings. By dividing the dimensions into subdimensions, it was possible to conduct within-exercise confirmatory factor analyses of assessor ratings. Results from these analyses were not consistent with prevailing halo error or general-impression explanations for the assessor rating process. This finding raises a number of interesting questions and suggests a possible fruitful direction for future research regarding assessor processes and the meaning of AC ratings.

Study Limitations

The primary limitation of the present study was the small sample size, especially with respect to postprogram multisource ratings. This led to low statistical power in most analyses, which may have obscured meaningful effects in some cases. The inclusion of participants from multiple organizations, although an advantage in many ways, introduced additional noise into the data set. Anecdotal comments from participants indicated that some participating organizations had cultures in which employee development was actively promoted but that other organizations provided little support or few development opportunities. It seems likely that differences in organizational factors may have had substantial impacts on participants' development, but these effects could not be directly tested due to the small number of participants from most organizations. The use of multisource feedback ratings to measure change is also problematic. Raters were not provided with any form of training or any incentive to rate accurately, and agreement between the three sources was low. Under such conditions, it is difficult to determine which measures are closest to true performance or improvement. Finally, although the present study addresses many of the types of possible validity evidence for DACs, it was not possible to address every type. For example, external measures of performance on the dimensions were not obtained, so the tests of convergent and discriminant relationships are limited, and organization-level data were not available to assess results criteria.

Conclusions and Suggestions for Future Research

Establishing that a DAC is both a valid assessment and an effective training intervention is difficult. Although some types of validity evidence are easily obtained, such as participant reactions and internal structure of assessor ratings, the critical questions of accuracy and improvement require data external to the DACs that are seldom available in practice. Measures of true job performance on the dimensions (or skills or tasks) of interest are needed to fully establish the accuracy of DAC ratings, and longitudinal on-the-job performance data are needed to measure improvement. The present study used multisource performance ratings to provide both types of information, but these ratings are often problematic (e.g., Byham, 2003) and it is not clear that their accuracy can be relied on. Measuring improvement over time is critical to the understanding of DACs, especially in light of the lack of systematic research regarding how much improvement can be expected and when.

The present study identifies a number of research needs in the effort to understand and apply DACs. First, the findings here regarding the internal structure of assessor ratings should be replicated and investigated further. As discussed, there are several possible explanations for these results, but the sample size here was insufficient to test them fully. Hierarchical models incorporating a common exercise factor and individual dimension factors may be the most appropriate way to describe the data, but such models require substantially larger samples. Second, the present study did not permit the investigation of convergent and discriminant relationships with external measures of the constructs or other variables. Though there is some evidence indicating that AC dimensions differ in their relationships with external constructs (e.g., Arthur et al., 2003), such evidence remains to be established for DACs. Third, as discussed, better longitudinal measures of on-the-job performance are needed to determine the effectiveness of DACs for catalyzing change. Longer-term measures are also desirable; the present study considered development within a window of 1 to 4 months, but it may take longer for changes in some dimensions to occur or to be perceived by a participant's coworkers. Fourth, detailed explorations of learning outcomes would provide insight into the development process involved in DACs. Kirkpatrick's (1976) taxonomy is extremely simple; recent research in this area has identified a whole host of potential learning outcomes that are worthy of investigation (e.g., Kraiger, 2002; Noe & Colquitt, 2002). Process analyses of the cognitive strategies used by participants in addressing the exercises (Kraiger et al., 1993) could be an especially fruitful direction for such research.

It is widely acknowledged that there are no typical ACs (Thornton & Rupp, 2005), and DACs vary widely in purpose, design, and implementation. To fully understand the effectiveness of the DAC method, studies are needed that consider a variety of exercise types, participants, dimensions (or tasks; see Lance et al., 2004), target jobs, target industries, and so on. However, the DACs in the present study were designed to synthesize current best practices for ACs and DACs with greater research control than is usually obtainable in organizational settings. Though other DACs may not share all the features of those discussed here (e.g., multiple feedback points, follow-up coaching), at least some of these elements are likely to be present in most cases, making the current results relevant to a variety of operational DACs. Consequently, the findings presented here represent an important first step in establishing validity evidence for the DAC method by suggesting a common framework by which such evidence can be meaningfully compiled and compared.

ACKNOWLEDGMENTS

Carra S. Sims is now at the Army Research Institute.

This research has been supported by the Douglas W. Bray and Ann Howard Award/Society for Industrial and Organizational Psychology Foundation, the State Farm Companies Foundation, the University of Illinois Campus Research Board, the University of Illinois at Urbana-Champaign Institute for Labor and Industrial Relations, and a National Science Foundation Graduate Research Fellowship.

This article is dedicated to George C. Thornton III, as his teaching, research, and mentoring have heavily inspired our work on this project.

The views, opinions, and findings contained in this article are solely those of the authors and should not be construed as reflecting the views of any of those units or agencies nor as an official Department of the Army or Department of Defense position, policy, or decision, unless so designated by other documentation.

Portions of this article were presented at the 20th annual meeting of the Society for Industrial and Organizational Psychology, Los Angeles, 2005, and at the 2004 International Congress on Assessment Center Methods, Las Vegas, Nevada.

We thank Silke Holub, Jean Drasgow, and Preeti Warty for their assistance with this project.

REFERENCES

Alliger, G. M., & Janak, E. A. (1989). Kirkpatrick's levels of training criteria: Thirty years later. *Personnel Psychology, 42*(2), 331–342.

American Educational Research Association, American Psychological Association, & American Council on Measurement in Education. (1999). *Standards for educational and psychological tests.* Washington, DC: American Psychological Association.

Arthur, W., Jr., Day, E. A., McNelly, T. L., & Edens, P. S. (2003). A meta-analysis of the criterion-related validity of assessment center dimensions. *Personnel Psychology, 56,* 125–54.

Atwater, L. E., Brett, J. F., & Ryan, J. M. (2004, April). *360 degree feedback to managers: Does it result in changes in employee attitudes?* Paper presented at the 19th annual meeting of the Society for Industrial and Organizational Psychology, Chicago.

Ballantyne, I., & Povah, N. (2004). *Assessment and development centres* (2nd ed). Aldershot, England: Gower.

Bentler, P. M., & Bonett, D. G. (1980). Significance tests and goodness of fit in the analysis of covariance structures. *Psychological Bulletin, 88,* 588–606.

Bhawuk, D. (2001). Evolution of culture assimilators: Toward theory-based assimilators. *International Journal of Intercultural Relations, 25,* 141–163.

Binning, J. F., & Barrett, G. V. (1989). Validity of personnel decisions: A conceptual analysis of the inferential and evidential bases. *Journal of Applied Psychology, 74,* 478–494.

Borman, W. C., & Brush, D. H. (1993). More progress toward a taxonomy of managerial performance requirements. *Human Performance, 6,* 1–21.

Bray, D. W., & Grant, D. L. (1966). The assessment center in the measurement of potential for business management. *Psychological Monographs, 80* (17, Whole No. 625), 1–27.

Brummel, B. J., & Spain, S. M. (2005, April). *Constructing parallel simulation exercises for developmental assessment centers.* Paper presented at the 20th annual meeting of the Society for Industrial and Organizational Psychology, Los Angeles.

Brush, D. H., & Licata, B. J. (1983). The impact of skill learnability on the effectiveness of managerial training and development. *Journal of Management, 9,* 27–39.

Byham, W. C. (2003, October). *Multirater/360° feedback—Does it produce better leaders?* Paper presented at the 31st International Congress on Assessment Center Methods, Atlanta, GA.

Carrick, P., & Williams, R. (1999). Development centres—A review of assumptions. *Human Resource Management Journal, 9,* 77–92.

Clapham, M. M., & Fulford, M. D. (1997). Age bias in assessment center ratings. *Journal of Managerial Issues, 9,* 373–387.

Cochran, D. S., Hinckle, T. W., & Dusenberry, D. (1987). Designing a developmental assessment center in a government agency: A case study. *Public Personnel Management, 16,* 145–152.

Colquitt, J. A., Conlon, D. E., Wesson, M. J., Porter, C. O. L. H., & Ng, K. Y. (2001). Justice at the millennium: A meta-analytic review of 25 years of organizational justice research. *Journal of Applied Psychology, 86,* 425–445.

Cronbach, L. J. (1989). Construct validation after thirty years. In R. L. Linn (Ed.), *Intelligence: Measurement, theory, and public policy: Proceedings of a symposium in honor of Lloyd G. Humphreys* (pp. 147–171). Champaign: University of Illinois.

Dulewicz, V., & Fletcher, C. (1982). The relationship between previous experience, intelligence, and background characteristics of participants and their performance in an assessment centre. *Journal of Occupational Psychology, 55,* 197–207.

Dunning, D. (1995). Trait importance and modifiability as factors influencing self-assessment and self-enhancement motives. *Personality and Social Psychology Bulletin, 21,* 1297–1306.

Dweck, C. S., & Leggett, E. L. (1988). A social-cognitive approach to motivation and personality. *Psychological Review, 95,* 256–273.

Engelbrecht, A. S., & Fischer, A. H. (1995). The managerial performance implications of a developmental assessment center process. *Human Relations, 48,* 387–404.

Gaugler, B. B., Rosenthal, D. B., Thornton, G. C., III, & Bentson, C. (1987). Meta-analysis of assessment center validity. *Journal of Applied Psychology, 72,* 493–511.

Griffiths, P., & Goodge, P. (1994). Development centres: The third generation. *Personnel Management, 26,* 40–43.

Haaland, S., & Christiansen, N. D. (2002). Implications of trait-activation theory for evaluating the construct validity of assessment center ratings. *Personnel Psychology, 55,* 137–163.

Hedge, J. W., & Kavanagh, M. J. (1988). Improving the accuracy of performance evaluations: Comparison of three methods of performance appraiser training. *Journal of Applied Psychology, 73,* 68–73.

Hellervik, L. W., Hazucha, J. F., & Schneider, R. J. (1992). Behavior change: Models, methods, and a review of evidence. In M. D. Dunnette & L. M. Hough (Eds.), *Handbook of industrial and organizational psychology* (Vol. 3, pp. 823–895). Palo Alto, CA: Consulting Psychologists Press.

Howard, A. (1997). A reassessment of assessment centers: Challenges for the 21st century. *Journal of Social Behavior and Personality, 12,* 13–52.

Huck, J. R., & Bray, D. W. (1976). Management assessment center evaluations and subsequent job performance of White and Black females. *Personnel Psychology, 29,* 13–30.

Hunter, R. A. (1990). Adding developmental value to assessment centres. *Occupational Psychologist, 12,* 17–20.

International Task Force on Assessment Center Guidelines. (2000). Guidelines and considerations for assessment center operations. *Public Personnel Management, 29,* 315–331.

Johnston, W. B. (1991). Global work force 2000: The new world labor market. *Harvard Business Review, 69,* 115–127.

Jones, R. G., & Whitmore, M. D. (1995). Evaluating developmental assessment centers as interventions. *Personnel Psychology, 48,* 377–388.

Kirkpatrick, D. L. (1967/1976). Evaluation of training. In R. L. Craig & L. R. Bittel (Eds.), *Training and development handbook* (Second Edition pp. 18-1–18-27. New York: McGraw-Hill.

Kluger, A. N., & DeNisi, A. (1996). Effects of feedback intervention on performance: A historical review, a meta-analysis, and a preliminary feedback intervention theory. *Psychological Bulletin, 119,* 254–284.

Kraiger, K. (2002). Decision-based evaluation. In K. Kraiger (Ed.), *Creating, implementing, and managing effective training and development: State-of-the-art lessons for practice* (pp. 331–375). San Francisco: Jossey-Bass.

Kraiger, K., Ford, J. K., & Salas, E. (1993). Application of cognitive, skill-based, and affective theories of learning outcomes into new methods of training evaluation. *Journal of Applied Psychology 78,* 311–328.

Lance, C. E., Lambert, T. A., Gewin, A. G., Lievens, F., & Conway, J. M. (2004). Revised estimates of dimension and exercise variance components in assessment center postexercise dimension ratings. *Journal of Applied Psychology, 89,* 377–385.

Lance, C. E., Newbolt, W. H., Gatewood, R. D., Foster, M. R., French, N. R., & Smith, D. E. (2000). Assessment center exercise factors represent cross-situational specificity, not method bias. *Human Performance, 13*, 323–353.

Landis, D., & Bhagat, R. S. (1996). A model of intercultural behavior and training. In D. Landis & R. S. Bhagat (Eds.), *Handbook of intercultural training* (2nd ed., pp. 1–13). Thousand Oaks, CA: Sage.

Lee, G., & Beard, D. (1994). *Development centres: Realizing the potential of your employees through assessment and development.* London: McGraw-Hill.

Lievens, F. (2001). Assessor training strategies and their effects on accuracy, interrater reliability, and discriminant validity. *Journal of Applied Psychology, 86*, 255–264.

Lievens, F. (2002). Trying to understand the different pieces of the construct validity puzzle of assessment centers: An examination of assessor and assessee effects. *Journal of Applied Psychology, 87*, 675–686.

Lievens, F., Chasteen, C. S., Day, E. A., & Christiansen, N. D. (2004, April). *Large-scale investigation of the role of trait activation theory for understanding assessment center convergent and discriminant validity.* Paper presented at the 19th annual conference of the Society for Industrial and Organizational Psychology, Chicago.

McCauley, C. D., & Hezlett, S. A. (2001). Individual development in the workplace. In N. Anderson, D. S. Ones, H. Sinangil, & C. Viswesveran, (Eds.), *Handbook of industrial, work, and organizational psychology: Vol.1. Personnel psychology* (pp. 313–335). London: Sage.

Messick, S. (1998). Test validity: A matter of consequence. *Social Indicators Research, 45*, 35–44.

Moses, J. L., & Boehm, V. R. (1975). Relationship of assessment-center performance to management progress of women. *Journal of Applied Psychology, 60*, 527–529.

Murphy, K. R., & Cleveland, J. N. (1995). *Understanding performance appraisal: Social, organizational, and goal-based perspectives.* Thousand Oaks, CA: Sage.

Noe, R. A., & Colquitt, J. A. (2002). Planning for training impact: Principles of training effectiveness. In K. Kraiger (Ed.), *Creating, implementing, and maintaining effective training and development: State-of-the-art lessons for practice* (pp. 53–79). San Francisco: Jossey-Bass.

Pulakos, E. D. (1984). A comparison of rater training programs: Error training and accuracy training. *Journal of Applied Psychology, 69*(4), 581–588.

Sackett, P. R. (1982). A critical look at some common beliefs about assessment centers. *Public Personnel Management, 11*, 140–147.

Sackett, P. R., & Tuzinski, K. (2001). The role of dimensions and exercises in assessment center judgments. In M. London (Ed.), *How people evaluate others in organizations* (pp. 111–129). Mahwah, NJ: Lawrence Erlbaum Associates, Inc.

Schleicher, D. J., Day, D. V., Mayes, B. T., & Riggio, R. E. (2002). A new frame for frame-of-reference training: Enhancing the construct validity of assessment centers. *Journal of Applied Psychology, 87*, 735–746.

Schmidt, F. L., & Hunter, J. E. (1998). The validity and utility of selection methods in personnel psychology: Practical and theoretical implications of 85 years of research findings. *Psychological Bulletin, 124*, 262–274.

Shore, T. H., Shore, L. M., & Thornton, G. C., III. (1992). Construct validity of self- and peer evaluations of performance dimensions in an assessment center. *Journal of Applied Psychology, 77*, 42–54.

Shore, T. H., Thornton, G. C., III, & Shore, L. M. (1990). Construct validity of two categories of assessment center dimension ratings. *Personnel Psychology, 43*, 101–116.

Smither, J. W., London, M., & Reilly, R. R. (2005). Does performance improve following multisource feedback? A theoretical model, meta-analysis, and review of empirical findings. *Personnel Psychology, 58*, 33–66.

Society for Industrial and Organizational Psychology. (2003). *Principles for the validation and use of personnel selection procedures* (4th ed.). Bowling Green, OH: Author.

Spychalski, A. C., Quiñones, M. A., Gaugler, B. B., & Pohley, K. (1997). A survey of assessment center practices in organizations in the United States. *Personnel Psychology, 50,* 71–90.

Tett, R. P., Guterman, H. A., Bleier, A., & Murphy, P. J. (2000). Development and content validation of a "hyperdimensional" taxonomy of managerial competence. *Human Performance, 13,* 205–251.

Thornton, G. C., III, & Byham, W. C. (1982). *Assessment centers and managerial performance.* New York: Academic Press.

Thornton, G. C., III, & Rogers, D. A. (2001, October). *Developmental assessment centers: Can we deliver the essential elements?* Paper presented at the 29th International Congress on Assessment Center Methods, Frankfurt, Germany.

Thornton, G. C., III, & Rupp, D. E. (2005). *Assessment centers in human resource management.* Mahwah, NJ: Lawrence Erlbaum Associates, Inc.

Tillema, H. H. (1998). Assessment of potential, from assessment centers to development centers. *International Journal of Selection and Assessment, 6,* 185–191.

Tucker, L. R., & Lewis, C. (1973). A reliability coefficient for maximum likelihood factor analysis. *Psychometrika, 38,* 1–10.

Waters, J. A. (1980). Managerial skill development. *Academy of Management Review, 5,* 449–453.

Zedeck, S., & Cascio, W. F. (1982). Performance appraisal decisions as a function of rater training and purpose of the appraisal. *Journal of Applied Psychology, 67,* 752–758.

Zuckerman, M., Gagne, M., & Nafshi, I. (2001). Pursuing academic interests: The role of implicit theories. *Journal of Applied Social Psychology, 31,* 2621–2631.

THE PSYCHOLOGIST-MANAGER JOURNAL, 2006, 9(2), 201–205

ᙀ II. NEW DIRECTIONS FOR ASSESSMENT CENTERS

A Commentary by Ann Howard

Ann Howard
Development Dimensions International

Fifty years after their corporate inauguration in AT&T's Management Progress Study (Howard & Bray, 1988), assessment centers (ACs) are now considered a classic tool for evaluating the skills and work behaviors of managers and other personnel. An international body has agreed on ACs' defining characteristics and requirements (International Task Force on Assessment Center Guidelines, 2000), and meta-analyses across a wide body of research have established their criterion-related validity (cf. Gaugler, Rosenthal, Thornton, III, Bentson, 1987).

Notwithstanding this coherence and consistency, a hallmark of ACs has been their plasticity. The characteristics they measure (usually job-relevant dimensions or competencies) and how they measure these characteristics (primarily in simulations) are uniquely defined for each AC application. This fundamental plasticity has kept ACs open to new populations, novel situations, and changes in work and organizational life.

KEY TRANSITIONS

ACs' historical path illustrates how their malleability ushered them into new arenas of practical use. In 1956 Douglas W. Bray created the business AC in order to study the lives and careers of Bell System managers. He defined 26 managerial dimensions; many of these, like planning and organizing and decision-making, are still in use today. To measure the dimensions he gathered multiple exercises, including precedent-setting simulations like an in-basket and leaderless group discussion.

Robert Greenleaf, the AT&T executive who hired Bray, thought that longitudinal research would inform the Bell System's selection and development programs. But before the first wave of data was collected for what became the 25-year Management Progress Study, it was clear that the method Bray used for the research would add value long before the knowledge it generated became generally available. Telephone company managers introduced to the AC saw its usefulness for selecting managers. Their first request for a practical application of the method was to identify which craft workers had the skills, motivations, and other characteristics to be effective first-level supervisors.

The transition from research to practice involved a simplification of the original assessment process. This included abandoning psychological tests and measures that required professional interpretation in favor of simulations, streamlining the number of dimensions to be measured, shifting the emphasis from clinical judgments to behavior, and training managers rather than psychologists to be assessors. These modifications made the AC much more accessible, and its success in identifying management potential led to its proliferation for other purposes.

Subsequent years saw ACs range across different types of organizations, from a few large corporations in the 1960s to a wide array of profit and non-profit organizations: business, education, hospitals, public safety, and many levels of federal and state governments. It also spread across organizational positions: middle and higher management in the early years, non-management personnel like empowered teams in the 1980s and consultative sales associates at the turn of the 21st century; and higher executives and CEOs in the late 20th and early 21st centuries. With each transition came new work challenges, new competencies, and new simulations to measure those competencies. For example, executive assessments often involve a media interview or the formulation and presentation of a new strategic direction for an organization or primary business unit.

Recent challenges to the plasticity of ACs concern the form in which they are presented to candidates. As organizational life has shifted away from paper correspondence to voice mail and e-mail messages, so too have AC simulations shifted from packets of paper defining each exercise to Web-based applications that simulate a modern day-in-the-life of an executive or other worker. The simulations are disaggregated, in that messages that might have constituted an original in-basket's items are interspersed with those providing background for meetings or other events that will occur during the assessment day. Participants complete the assessment using a simulated desktop on their computers, where each move can be electronically measured. Telephone or in-person role-plays and recorded voice messages allow additional data collection. As in real life, individuals allot their own time to the various challenges, and the manner in which they do this is one of the things measured. Web-based ACs allow participants to participate remotely rather than in person, and they provide assessors with administrative efficiencies as well as computer-aided scoring.

WHY ASSESSMENT CENTERS?

Although experience has shown that ACs can be readily adapted to new purposes, a practical person might wonder whether it's worthwhile to do so. Despite greater efficiency in today's Web-based designs, ACs are costly to develop and administer. Given that there are other valid but inexpensive personnel selection tools, such as cognitive tests, personality inventories, or biographical data forms, why bother with complex ACs?

The explanation is that ACs bring advantages that rival tools cannot match. Simulations are unique in their ability to showcase participants' skills. Unlike tests, no inferences need to be made about behavior; participants demonstrate what they can do within the simulation process. Although it might be argued that multi-rater surveys also rely on evaluations of live behavior, survey respondents lack the careful training and calibration that assessors receive to assure reliable and accurate ratings. Moreover, survey respondents have only observed behavior in the current job, but simulations provide an opportunity to observe behavior in future positions.

Because of their ability to peer into the future, ACs may have their greatest pay-off in evaluating people for new roles. For leaders, prime opportunities for assessment are at important thresholds: the initial move into management, advancement from a tactical to an operational role, or moving from operational responsibility to setting strategy. Similarly, organizations promoting major cultural or strategic changes—from traditional to empowered teams, or from transactional to consultative selling—have capitalized on ACs' ability to measure performance in new roles.

ACs also offer many advantages to participants. They provide a realistic preview of a future position that can help people recognize whether it is a good fit to their interests, motivations, and talents. Participants readily see simulations' job relevance, and they view them as fairer ways to showcase their skills than techniques like tests or biographical measures whose relevance is far less transparent (Hausknecht, Day, & Thomas, 2004). Adverse impact is smaller for ACs than for cognitive tests and negligible for measures of interpersonal skills (Howard & Bray, 1988). Perhaps most important, ACs elicit behaviors that can be used for meaningful and credible feedback.

NEW DIRECTIONS

The more an organization hopes to gain from its evaluation of managerial or other personnel, the more likely that it will need an AC. If the purpose is raw prediction, that is, selecting the most promising candidates from a large pool of untried applicants and making no further use of the information, organizations can find less expensive tools that will maximize a validity coefficient. But the more the organization needs to know about a candidate—as which position or team he/she will best fit, or which roles are most likely to cause him/her the most difficulties—the more advantages an AC brings.

ACs stand out among other evaluation methods in their ability to diagnose participants' strengths and development needs for target roles. The output of the center provides a behavioral roadmap for shoring up flagging competencies and capitalizing on stronger ones. Research has shown that organizations with high quality leader development programs and formal succession management programs have superior business performance (Bernthal & Wellins, 2005). It should be no surprise, then, that more and more organizations are using ACs not just for selection, but also for development (Spychalski, Quiñones, Gaugler, & Pohley, 1997).

If development is a critical need, and if ACs are such a fine tool to guide development, then why not make ACs part of the development process itself? This new direction for ACs is precisely what is explored in this journal issue. The developmental AC, or DAC, is a learning tool, a mirror that lets assessees see their own behavior in action. Guided by feedback from professional assessors, developmental assessment center trainees have an opportunity to practice new behaviors in parallel assessment exercises before trying them out in real-life situations.

The articles in this volume provide clear and compelling explanations of how a DAC can be implemented and the value it can bring. Besides giving ACs a new purpose, the authors also suggest re-evaluation and augmentation of the dimensions to be assessed. This point is critical. The purpose of the AC (selection, diagnosis, or development) should drive the types of dimensions measured, just as the nature of each dimension should drive how it is measured.

Following the AC tradition initiated by the Management Progress Study, these articles build on research. The plasticity of ACs cries out for research to demonstrate that variations and innovations capitalize on the method's strengths without sacrificing its measurement foundations. These articles tie their new direction to relevant research and theory and present new evidence on the perceived developability of dimensions as well as the efficacy of DACs for promoting behavior change.

ACKNOWLEDGMENTS

It is particularly gratifying that the authors' research in this issue was supported by a grant from the SIOP Foundation's Douglas W. Bray-Ann Howard Fund. The Fund's intent is to encourage and support worthwhile research on ACs and managerial or leadership development. These initial grant recipients have provided assurance that the Fund is serving its purpose and will hopefully encourage others to apply.

REFERENCES

Bernthal, P. R., & Wellins, R. S. (2005). *Leadership Forecast 2005/2006: Best Practices for Tomorrow's Global Leaders.* Pittsburgh: Development Dimensions International.

Gaugler, B. B., Rosenthal, D. B., Thornton, G. C., III, & Bentson, C. (1987). Meta-analysis of assessment center validity. *Journal of Applied Psychology, 74,* 611–618.

Hausknecht, J. P., Day, D. V., & Thomas, S. C. (2004). Applicant reactions to selection procedures: An updated model and meta-analysis. *Personnel Psychology, 57,* 639–683.

Howard, A., & Bray, D. W. (1988). *Managerial lives in transition: Advancing age and changing times.* New York: Guilford Press.

International Task Force on Assessment Center Guidelines (2000, May 4). *Guidelines and Ethical Considerations for Assessment Center Operations.* Endorsed by 28th International Congress on Assessment Center Methods. www.assessmentcenters.org/pdf/00guidelines.pdf.

Spychalski, A. C., Quiñones, M. A., Gaugler, B. B., & Pohley, K. (1997). A survey of assessment center practices in organizations in the United States. *Personnel Psychology, 50,* 71–90.

THE PSYCHOLOGIST-MANAGER JOURNAL, 2006, 9(2), 207–209
Copyright © 2006 by the Society of Psychologists in Management

₥ III. BOOK REVIEW AND COMMENTARY

International Assignments: An Integration of Strategy, Research, & Practice,
by Linda K. Stroh, Mark E. Mendenhall, J. Stewart Black, and Hal B. Gregersen.
Mahwah, NJ: Lawrence Erlbaum Associates, 2005, pp. 304, $89.95 cloth, $39.95
paper.

Reviewed by
Sherry K. Schneider
University of West Florida

As an expatriate who lived and worked in Australia for almost 7 years, I was looking forward to reading Stroh, Black, Mendenhall and Gregersen's new book, *International Assignments: An Integration of Strategy, Research, and Practice*
(2005). What I immediately learned was that the audience for this book is not people like me, but managers who hire people like me for international assignments.
Although this book was published too late to help me, I think most international
employees would benefit greatly if employers took the advice of Stroh and her
other colleagues to heart.

Given the competitiveness of the global market, this book is a timely addition to
the bookshelf of the human resource manager or executive. Stroh et al. cite statistics (Black & Gregerson, 1999, cited on p. 14) that 10% to 20% of U.S. expats return early from assignments, with each failed effort costing their employers from
$300,000 to $1 million. Furthermore, the authors estimate that an average 4-year
assignment costs companies from $1 million to $3.5 million. About 25% of executives leave the company within 2 years of return from overseas. Through failed assignments and turnover after repatriation, there is a one in five chance that the company who sent the expatriate abroad will not receive any benefits from this sizable
expenditure. Finally, the authors stress that the outcomes of poor preassignment
planning and repatriation are not just failed projects or disgruntled executives. Lost

Correspondence should be sent to Sherry K. Schneider, Department of Psychology, University of
West Florida, 11000 University Parkway, Pensacola, FL 32514-5751. E-mail: sschneider@uwf.edu

opportunities for the organization to grow and develop its leadership potential in international strategic planning may be the greatest loss to the organization.

The book is broken into four sections: an introduction, Before the Assignment, During the Assignment, and After the Assignment. The introduction includes chapters on strategic management and cross-cultural adjustment. The second section covers selection and training. The third section deals with adjustment, appraisal, and compensation, while the final section discusses the issues relating to repatriation. In my view, the strength of this book is in its emphasis on laying the groundwork before the assignment (especially in selection) and dealing with the aftermath of repatriation. It is in these two aspects that international assignments differ markedly from traditional employment. The authors do an admirable job reviewing the relevant literature concerning why selection for international assignments should be based on more than specific technical or professional abilities. In addition to technical expertise, candidates for international assignments must have excellent communication skills that include a genuine willingness to communicate with host-country nationals. Language skills, social skills, lack of ethnocentricity, and flexibility are also important traits for an expat manager. The book mentions several methods for assessing these criteria, including biographical data, work samples, and a standardized test called the Global Assignment Preparedness Survey, developed by the authors themselves.

Other benefits of the book include specific recommendations on training, compensation, and logistical support during and after the assignment. The book is filled with interesting cases and examples. A highlight for me was the chapter on managing expatriate dual allegiances to the host and parent firm, including a discussion of the pros and cons of managers who "go native" versus those who "leave their hearts at home" or are "dual citizens" (p. 137).

There are some topics that I would have liked to see covered more thoroughly. The authors acknowledge the important role of the spouse and family in the executive's willingness to accept an overseas assignment and in the executive's ultimate ability to adjust successfully to that assignment. More of the book could have been devoted to the research and practice on this crucial topic.

In general, the depth of coverage of topics in a book such as this one is a difficult challenge that requires reviewing the academic literature, providing relevant examples, and distilling practical advice from both. For the most part, the authors succeed at this delicate balancing act. As an academic, I found myself wishing for more specifics on the research described. On the other hand, I can imagine that practicing managers might be frustrated by the lack of detail offered for some of the recommendations. A resource guide included as an appendix or as a companion website would address these minor concerns. For example, how to obtain the Global Assignment Preparedness Survey selection instrument cited in the text would have been useful. The citation for this instrument was also missing from the reference section at the back of the book. Such a resource guide would make the book much more useful to practicing managers.

These are small gripes, however. I applaud Lawrence Erlbaum Associates for publishing a book written by academic experts in international management for practicing managers. I understand that a similar book published by Lawrence Erlbaum Associates on human resources for the non–HR manager (Kulik, 2004) has sold quite well. It is imperative that as psychologist-managers we support publishers who educate managers based on research and best practice. George Miller, in his famous 1969 American Psychological Association presidential address (as cited in Fowler, 1999), made a plea to researchers to "give psychology away" by sharing their findings in a way that the general public could understand and benefit from them. Kudos to the authors and publishers of this book for giving psychology away for the benefit of practicing international managers.

REFERENCES

Black, S., & Gregersen, H. B. (1999). The right way to manage expats. *Harvard Business Review, 77*(2), 52–63.

Fowler, R. D. (1999). Giving psychology away. *APA Monitor, 30.* Retrieved April 24, 2006, from http://apa.org/monitor/may99/rc.html

Kulik, C. (2004). *Human resources for the non-HR manager.* Mahwah, NJ: Lawrence Erlbaum Associates, Inc.

Stroh, L. K., Black, J. S., Mendenhall, M. E., & Gregersen, H. B. (2005). *International assignments: An integration of strategy, research, and practice.* Mahwah, NJ: Lawrence Erlbaum Associates, Inc.

THE PSYCHOLOGIST-MANAGER JOURNAL, 2006, 9(2), 211–214

Ψ IV. LAST PAGE

The Last Page: A Gentle Shove?
Thoughts About Assessment

Rosemary Hays-Thomas
Editor

This issue of *The Psychologist-Manager Journal* focuses on assessment centers (ACs) used to measure job-related attributes for purposes of employee selection and development. Psychologist-managers will be familiar with the origin and widespread use of ACs as one means of measuring the strengths and shortcomings of candidates for employment or advancement, and this issue extends the literature on ACs to a new function in organizations: employee development.

Assessment has been on my mind recently, partly because my institution has recently undergone its decennial reaffirmation of accreditation, and we have been developing an extensive system to develop and assess learning outcomes in the context of an initiative in the state of Florida. Lately, however, I have seen some worrisome reminders that the rhetoric of assessment involves political and economic motivations; unrealistic assumptions and expectations; and a superficial understanding of the theory, procedures, and limitations of testing.

For example, a recent article (Cohen & Rosenzweig, 2006, para. 4 in online version) argued that multiple-choice tests were coming to "the brink of obsolescence" because students could easily find the right answers by searching the Internet with their cell phones. The article portrayed multiple-choice questions as speedy, cheap, and incapable of testing anything other than rote memory of facts. The authors were not psychometricians or test developers, and I found myself arguing with their logic and their understanding of testing, but their views are probably widely held.

Assessment is in the zeitgeist. Bill Siegfried's introduction to this issue points out some manifestations of this in public elementary and secondary education and

Correspondence should be sent to Rosemary Hays-Thomas, Department of Psychology, University of West Florida, 11000 University Parkway, Pensacola, FL 32514. E-mail: rlowe@uwf.edu

in higher education. The federal No Child Left Behind Act, with its mandated high-stakes testing, is the focus of frequent commentary in local and national media, and in an attempt to improve children's education many states have developed their own programs that include standardized testing. The chairman of the federal Commission on the Future of Higher Education, Charles Miller, has predicted that in an effort to justify public funding and tuition increases, "early movers and best practices" will lead to the promotion of testing as the best way to show the value added by the college experience. "We need to give [this process] a gentle shove," he wrote (as cited in Field, 2006, para. 4 in online version). The commission will not mandate testing but will recommend two standardized tests. In short order, two organizations representing publicly funded colleges and universities also recommended that their members "develop their own voluntary approach that would allow the public to compare similar institutions" (Schmidt & Selingo, 2006, p. A33). Many in higher education administration believe that if institutions do not move in this direction voluntarily, a system of standardized testing will be imposed on them, as it has on public elementary and secondary education. Consistent with promoting this view, regional accrediting agencies emphasize the importance of data-based decision making that makes use of assessments of desired outcomes, particularly student learning. Meanwhile, faculty—who spend much of their time preparing and grading tests and other assessments—wonder why it is that so many outside the classroom seem to believe that colleges do not assess their students' learning.

A headline in the *Chronicle of Higher Education* read, "Government analyst says shoddy statistics tell a false tale about higher education" (Glenn, 2006). Clifford Adelman, a senior research analyst at the U.S. Department of Education, was quoted as saying, "We have an obligation to prevent statistical representations from turning into propaganda" (p. 31). Adelman charged journalists, legislators, and others with dissemination of obviously "shoddy" statistics about outcomes such as graduation rates and grade inflation. For example, reported graduation rates often do not take into account those who transfer and graduate from a different institution.

The Associated Press recently reported that many states are able to report misleadingly positive results from the No Child Left Behind Act by excluding scores from ethnic and other minority groups that are "too small to count" (Bass, Dizon, & Feller, 2006, p. 4A). Draconian penalties for repeated failure by any student category encourage such creative strategies for meeting the letter but not the spirit of the law. Critics of No Child Left Behind argue that its mandated testing encourages "teaching to the test" and a diversion of time and resources from important subject areas that are not covered by the test, such as civics or physical education. I recently received a handout at a public meeting that stated that the advertised goal of No Child Left Behind is for 100% of students to be "proficient" by 2013–2014. However, in Florida, proficiency in reading for third graders is defined by scoring at or above the 51st percentile (Hamilton, 2006). It seems that only in Lake Woebegone and in Florida can all students be "above average." Apparently, someone does not understand the difference between percent and percentage, between criterion-referenced and norm-referenced assessment. Misunderstanding or misuse of statistics is not new, but it is very discouraging.

As seen in the national news, various constituencies are assessing the effectiveness of many public policies and governmental responsibilities, most recently the federal response to hurricanes Katrina and Rita and the operation of the Federal Emergency Management Association. Assessment can clearly play an important role in institutional improvement and in decisions that affect individuals and organizations. But it seems that assessment also has a political purpose: When you think something isn't working, then assess it.

Most of these examples come from educational contexts, but I do not doubt that similar problems are found in other organizational settings. A particularly telling example is offered by Muchinsky (2004), who described a common preference among managers for hiring applicants with raw or percentile scores of 90 or higher, without regard for the norm group or the number of questions. Muchinsky traced this preference to experience in elementary and high school with scores of 90 earning a grade of A and the reasonable desire of managers to hire "A-level performers." Consistent with my worries about the rhetoric of assessment is McDaniel's "expression of concern" (2006) about some employment testing; in his article, he decried "inappropriate reporting practices" and "claims [for testing] unsupported by data" (p. 39).

Of course psychologist-managers who develop or use assessments in organizations are ethically bound to do whatever is possible to ensure that tests are appropriately used and interpreted (Lowman, 2006). Acknowledging the ethical obligations of professional psychologists, McDaniel (2006) raised the additional question of how to enforce standards of good testing practice in organizational settings. And in a thoughtful case study of the organizational change involved with the development and use of a new testing program, Muchinsky (2004) argued for more attention in journals to issues of implementation. He identified 10 issues in the process of an actual test development project that illustrated the meeting of psychometric principles with organizational realities, and he provided recommendations for maintaining psychometric integrity while responding effectively to human and organizational concerns.

At least two conclusions flow from this discussion. First, those who have some understanding of the uses and limitations of assessment can and should share this understanding in public and organizational settings when measurement and statistics are misused or abused. I quote the second conclusion, with thanks to Bill Siegfried, who as special issue editor commented to me the following after reading a draft of this commentary.

When we talk about assessment, it is usually in the context of evaluating an outcome. We test children in schools to determine whether or not the school has met a standard.

We may test higher education institutions to see how they compare (with others, or with standards). We assess Federal hurricane responses to document the failures. Assessment has become synonymous with evaluation, and in the hands of untrained consumers who stand to benefit or lose, the information is often misused, either intentionally or unintentionally. Lost in all of this is that assessment can serve other, more noble roles. Instead of testing school children to determine whether their school is up to standard, we can assess the children to see what they should learn. Perhaps higher education institutions should be compared on how much their students develop in the course of 4 years. Maybe the most successful organization is the one that hires the B performers and trains them to reach the top. The history of ACs is no different—we tout their success in employee selection while downplaying their potential for employee development. One contribution of this issue of the journal is that it highlights the importance of assessment for development, in contrast to the more common use of assessment to make a judgment about success.

Finally, I have reflected on Muchinsky's article (2004) from the perspective of editor of a journal whose readers are predominantly practitioners. I invite each of you to consider how you might contribute to a literature of implementation in psychology and management by writing in our pages about your experiences in joining theory and practice. Stories of success and of learning through nonsuccess are equally welcome because *The Psychologist-Manager Journal* seeks to provide articles that are of interest and use to our readership. This invitation is a gentle shove for professional service through literary mentoring of future psychologist-managers.

REFERENCES

Bass, F., Dizon, N. Z., & Feller, B. (2006, April 18). Loopholes in act leave some children behind. *Pensacola News-Journal,* p. 4A.

Cohen, D. J., & Rosenzweig, R. (2006). No computer left behind. *Chronicle of Higher Education.* Retrieved April 27, 2006, from http://chronicle.com/weekly/v52/i25/25b00601.htm

Field, K. (2006). Panel to give colleges "gentle shove" toward testing. *Chronicle of Higher Education.* Retrieved on April 27, 2006, from http://chronicle.com/weekly/v52/i31/31a03301.htm

Glenn, D. (2006, April 21). Government analyst says shoddy statistics tell a false tale about higher education. *Chronicle of Higher Education,* p. A31.

Hamilton, J. (2006, April 22). *The No Child Left Behind Act of 2001: Key state and district issues for Florida.* Material distributed at a public meeting in Pensacola, FL.

Lowman, R. L. (Ed.). (2006). *The ethical practice of psychology in organizations* (2nd ed.). Washington, DC: American Psychological Association.

McDaniel, M. A. (2006). Expression of concern. *Industrial-Organizational Psychologist, 43*(4), 39–40.

Muchinsky, P. (2004). When the psychometrics of test development meets organizational realities: A conceptual framework for organizational change, examples, and recommendations. *Personnel Psychology, 57,* 175–209.

Schmidt, P., & Selingo, J. (2006, April 21). Groups ask colleges to measure learning. *Chronicle of Higher Education,* p. A33.

THE PSYCHOLOGIST-MANAGER JOURNAL, 2006, 9(2), 215

Acknowledgment of Reviewers

The Editor would like to thank the following individuals for the assistance they have provided in reviewing manuscripts submitted to *The Psychologist-Manager Journal*. Their generosity, expertise, and professionalism are very much appreciated.

— Rosemary Hays-Thomas,
Editor

Kenneth Ball	Steven J. Kass	Sherry K. Schneider
Gayle Baugh	Laura L. Koppes	William D. Siegfried, Jr.
John Bilbrey	Thomas J. Kramer	Marion A. Terenzio
John M. Cornwell	John Langhorne	I. Marlene Thorn
Blake A. Frank	Rodney L. Lowman	Nancy T. Tippins
Marilyn K. Gowing	Joseph E. McGrath	Stephen J. Vodanovich
Carl I. Greenberg	Edward J. Pavur	Susan E. Walch
Leslie B. Hammer	Jill N. Reich	
Albert R. Hollenbeck	Linda M. Richardson	

T - #0149 - 270225 - C0 - 229/152/8 - PB - 9780805893465 - Gloss Lamination